CONSCIOUS
THE ART OF BEING

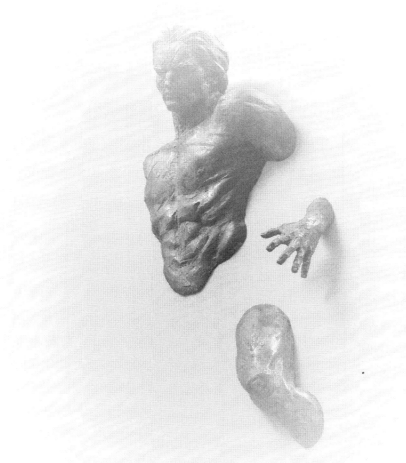

CONSCIOUS
THE ART OF BEING

YISROEL ROLL

WITH MICHAEL LOCKMAN

ISBN 978-1721555130
Copyright © 2018 by Yisroel Roll

Front Cover Art: Matteo Pugliese,
"Tra due mondi" Between two worlds,
2009 Bronze Sculpture
Photo Credit: Claudio Cipriani

For Dr. Jeffrey and
Dr. Chris Lafferman
Your personal and professional
integrity is matched only by your
sincere desire to heal broken lives

Contents

From Awake to Conscious

We are awake, but not conscious. We walk, talk, work, eat, play and live, but many of us are not living consciously. We go through the motions, and life happens without any real living going on. We "do" but we fail "to be."

The definition of conscious is: *aware of and responding to one's surroundings; as in "the patient is conscious." This includes being awake and aware of people, place and time.*

This aspect of the definition means that you can be awake, but passive. You can be aware of your surroundings but you may be responding with passive complacency, as if you are a casual observer of your environment.

There is a second dimension of the definition of conscious, as follows: *deliberate, intentional; as in "A conscious effort to walk properly."* The synonyms for this dimension of conscious are: *intended, purposeful, purposive, knowing, considered, calculated, willful, premeditated, planned and volitional.*

This latter aspect of consciousness is what this book is

about: How to transform being passively awake into becoming deliberately purposeful. In other words, this book will teach you how to live consciously and take control of your life.

In my professional psychotherapy practice, I lead group therapy sessions in a public mental health clinic where many of the clients are on public disability or welfare, and suffer from severe anxiety, bipolar disorder, schizophrenia, substance abuse and PTSD. Many are recovering addicts, and were physically, emotionally and sexually abused as children and teenagers. In my private practice, I see middle-class clients who work in white color jobs, have nuclear families and suffer from depression, anxiety and Attention Deficit Disorder. In both of my clinics, there is a common denominator—people are not aware of, or "forget" their strengths or "who they are" and are merely surviving; they just try to keep their heads above water.

Rhonda was a nurse for 22 years. She always had anxiety but it got worse when her mother died, her boyfriend left her and she was evicted from her apartment, all in the course of one month. She became Manic/Depressive where she stayed up for 48 hours straight and then slept for 24 hours. She did this for a few months. She lost her job and was forced to go on welfare. She started living in a broken down RV with no running water and a broken roof. She was in and out of hospital psychiatric wards. She forgot her abilities and her strengths. She forgot who she was.

At our clinic, Rhonda was prescribed medication to address the bipolar imbalance. The optimum treatment for mental health disorders is the dual treatment of medication and talk therapy. During group therapy in our clinic Rhonda discovered that she lacked self awareness of her abilities; she stopped being conscious of her "self."

Elizabeth is a neurosurgeon at a prominent hospital. She has performed 2,000 brain surgeries over a twenty five year career and has a wonderful bedside manner. She has always been conscientious and a perfectionist. After all, you need to be pretty perfect when you perform neurosurgery. After 25 years as a successful surgeon she developed severe anxiety and panic attacks and began to freeze during surgery, fearing that she would make a mistake. She came to my private practice for help.

Rhonda and Elizabeth are awake but not conscious. What happened?

The core self is made up of a cognitive awareness of your strengths and abilities. When you are conscious you can analyze a challenge or situation and cognitively access the toolbox of resources you have to solve or deal with the problem. Then you can proactively figure out which one of your strengths you can draw upon to deal with the challenge. However, if life has dealt you a painful hand of physical, emotional or sexual abuse, and you develop anxiety and depression due to unresolved emotional pain, then your cognitive agility and resilience become lethargic, stuck or frozen. You lose confidence and self-esteem. You stop believing in yourself because you lose touch with your inner abilities, resources and awareness of who you really are. You feel beaten down and unable to deal with the problem. You remain awake but you are not conscious.

Due to the fact that you have never processed or come to terms with the abuse you suffered as a child, adolescent or young adult, your core self gets covered in layers of emotional pain. The layers of pain make you feel anxious, and depressed as if you have lost the ability to respond to the difficulty you are currently facing. The current stressor, i.e. the death of a loved one, an abusive relationship, or the loss of a job, triggers memories and palpable emotional feelings of your earlier traumatic experience. It feels like the trauma is raw and happening all over again, in a different form and context and with different players. You feel overwhelmed and begin to despair. You interpret the challenges that you are currently facing as overwhelming and you feel existentially lonely—like you are the only one with this problem and you cannot possibly get out of it. You feel trapped and unable to move.

Anxiety, depression and loneliness cause a disconnection from the world and from yourself. Even when surrounded by others—sometimes especially then—this disconnect can be paralyzing, and can lead to a sense of emptiness, isolation and alienation from your "self." Ultimately, self-worth and self-esteem are the casualties of anxiety, depression and loneliness, which we will call ADL (anxiety, depression loneliness,) and make you feel unworthy of love.

Pervasive ADL can also erode your sense of identity, leading to a state of dissociation, which leads to a detachment from your own thoughts, memories, surroundings, and and purpose. This impaired self-awareness contributes to a sense of worthlessness. A cycle begins of going to sleep depressed, and waking the next morning frightened and overwhelmed at the prospect of the day.

Often, these psychological symptoms lead to lethargy and physical weakness, and, without vital physical or emotional energy, you reach a point while evaluating your options—perhaps even your life—and find yourself asking, *Well, what's the point?*

The inner emotional turmoil that ADL engenders may lead us to numb the pain with opiates, alcohol, or other substances; or it may create the urge to "give up" for the pain is too great to bear. When we lose the connection to our inner feeling of being "alive," we feel existentially empty and become trapped within our inner despair. We lose connection to our inner humanity and our existence becomes devoid of substance; we simply go through the motions and live in a spiritual vacuum. We drift aimlessly in this inner emptiness and lose touch with a truly grounded sense of self.[1]

It is easy to believe that ADL is something that happens *to* you, and, therefore, that you have no control over it. The truth—which we will explore together in this book—is that you are faced with a real choice when things happen to you: you can give in to ADL—and experience feelings of detachment, rejection, alienation, and powerlessness,—or you can recognize this state of being as an opportunity for *aloneness*, which we define as a proactive, purposeful journey into your psyche. When you make your *"aloneness"* work for you, it stops being considered a noun; rather, *aloneness* becomes a "verb." When you use your aloneness as a tool for self-discovery, you embark on a process of becoming conscious.

When you are conscious and aware of your true value

---

1   Kagan, J. The Jewish Self, Targum Press, Jerusalem, 1999. p. 14-21

you awaken your innate worth and competence and activate your sense of resilience and vitality. You feel once again the exhilaration of a profound closeness to another human being, and when you see a beautiful landscape you experience a moment of inner peace. You become centered within your deeper inner being and you regain a sense of radical uniqueness.[2] You come alive again.

Aloneness forces you to examine and reflect upon your deepest thoughts and fears. When you muster the courage to face your deepest fears and pain, you will encounter your unique essence. Surprisingly, your darkest moments of *aloneness* teach you what you are about, and, ultimately, give you the power to let go of seeking and needing acceptance and approval from others. This is a journey that will give you the key to self-acceptance. In this state of existential aloneness, alone against the world, you discover your "self," and the meaning of your life. This is called consciousness.

Before you can achieve this, however, you must understand that how you *interpret* the circumstances that brought you to ADL is far more powerful than the circumstances themselves. Whether the challenging stimulus or circumstance is an event, a trauma, or a state of mind, the most common "spin" or interpretation that we place on it is, *This has separated/detached/ disconnected me from the world and others. I am alone, abandoned, and rejected.* Circumstances, however, have no motives, agendas, or fixed outcomes of their own: it is how you *understand* them that gives them meaning.

---

2   Kagan, J. ibid.

If you interpret a challenging event as negative or painful, it is this interpretation—not the circumstance—which creates a negative, painful reality. From within that reality, it is easy to conclude that the world is against you. This interpretation is understandable because you are driven by your emotional self. When something or someone opposes, disapproves, or does not accept or love you, it is natural to feel rejected, abandoned and alone. Left unchecked, these feelings will lead to severe anxiety and depression, and even a feeling of physical/emotional pain, such that life becomes very hard to bear.

In order to understand and come to terms with your anxiety, depression and loneliness, (ADL) and how to heal from it, we must ask: is loneliness a *feeling* or a *state of mind?* The answer dictates the approach.

We have three dimensions of self:

1. The Physical—the part of the conscious self which interfaces with the body, namely instinct, impulse, the brain, the intellect, memory and imagination;

2. The Emotional—emotional appreciation of the aesthetic—art, music, harmony and experiencing feelings of love, happiness, sadness, fear, anger and frustration;

3. Conscious Intellect—the part of the self which exercises Free Will and chooses to pursue truth, wisdom and moral values.

If ADL is a *state of mind,* the circumstances leading to that state of mind must be re-examined and, if possible, reinterpreted. For example, being rejected by one's peers:

a sense of not "fitting in". This may cue a sense of detachment, making loneliness and depression seem inevitable: in this way, anxiety, depression and loneliness are a state of mind. If, however, you understand that same rejection as a freedom from the strictures of conformity, you are instead given the opportunity to be unique, and—by these same circumstances—your world does not shrink into isolation and alienation, rather it can expand through expression and individuality.

If ADL is a *feeling*, healing will follow from behavior. There is a close and causal relationship between what you do and what you feel. This is based on the concept called cognitive dissonance, meaning that your feelings catch up with your actions. If you act positively, you feel positive. If you see yourself as connected to others and as a giver, you feel more connected, become more connected, and anxiety, depression and loneliness lose their root within. The way to rise above emotional neediness is to graduate from approval seeking. As children, we need approval from parents and authority figures, not only to feel good about ourselves, but for our basic freedoms. We need this approval as children because we have no sense of self, or the capability for self-reflection. Only feedback and "reflected appraisals" from parents can tell us whether or not we are doing well, and, indeed, who we are.

We have all grown up chronologically, but often, we do not graduate from that emotional need for acceptance. For any number of reasons, many people continue to turn to authority figures for feedback rather than developing and, eventually, trusting their ability to self-evaluate. Armed with an independent sense of self and identity, you discover that you no longer need the acceptance, or approval, of others. More importantly, you come to understand that looking to others to "tell" you who you are, or to ratify how you choose to live your life, is nothing more or less than emotional slavery. Gaining a sense of self leads to a personal redemption; an exodus from emotional enslavement. This is the birth of consciousness.

The ultimate graduation from approval-seeking occurs when you gain a consciousness that you are here for a unique reason and mission that only you can achieve. If you learn to approve of *yourself,* then you no longer need approval from parents, teachers or friends. You are now liberated from approval seeking, and take on a world-view of making a contribution to society and your environment; you focus on "making a difference."

It does not matter if people approve of you, or not (as long as you act appropriately and in accordance with moral values). Life is not a popularity contest. You are here to accomplish something by making a contribution to society and to the lives of others. With this new mindset and approach to life, you can graduate from approval-seeking to contribution.

The fact that you are alone does not mean that you have to be lonely. Rather, it means that you are unique in the world in that you can make a unique contribution to the world. Aloneness, therefore, in its purest form, means to give of yourself to others and to society; in others words, to serve.

The gift of *aloneness* contains within itself the inner consciousness needed to stand up for yourself through individuality, independence, and wholeness.

The word "alone" refers to existential aloneness—which surprisingly, leads to tranquility. When something is alone it has no opposition, and therefore it finds uniqueness and tranquility within itself. It becomes "self" contained.

We usually think of *aloneness* as a negative state that leads to emotional loneliness. Many people suffer from loneliness, and it is debilitating. But a Conscious Aloneness leads to inner serenity when you become alone and one: integrated within yourself. This means accepting your *aloneness* and uniqueness as a mission to give, serve and contribute. When you become conscious of the fact that you are here for a unique reason and that you can and do make a difference, then your aloneness is transformed into Conscious Solitude. As one client, who had attempted suicide and came to our clinic said, "in my nothingness, I discovered somethingness."

Of course you are alone: you, alone, have been sent into the world on a unique mission to make a unique contribution. You can transform feelings of alienation and isolation into an awareness of your unique singularity. Not lonely, but "only." "Only you," instead of lonely you.

Aloneness means singularity and indivisibility, It speaks to the positive dimensions of aloneness meaning uniqueness and individuality.

With this awareness and consciousness, *aloneness* can be explored and mapped for its potential: it can contribute to your sense of fulfillment, rather than wrongfully conflated with loneliness, or misconstrued as a depressing mindset or a condition outside of your control.

To find your true *self* is to become conscious of your innate goodness which will lead to your actualizing your unique, positive character traits, which will, in turn lead to healthier self-esteem. In fact, you will discover something more fundamental than self-esteem; you will discover your conscious self. This book will teach you how to achieve consciousness, and how to get good at the art of *being*.

Conscious Therapy

O ne of the prerequisites to acquire a *conscious self* is an accurate self-evaluation in order to assess how to react to and navigate the particular life challenge that you are currently facing. In order to cognitively and emotionally assess who you "are," and thereby develop your self-concept, take an inventory of your:

1. Physical and material assets, e.g. physical attributes and material possessions;
2. Activities and capabilities, e.g. hobbies and talents;
3. Social and psychological characteristics, e.g. manners, habits, dispositions;
4. Philosophical beliefs, e.g. moral values and political views.
5. Character traits: your personality attributes, i.e. leadership, perseverance, consistency, compassion, giving, empathy, sensitivity, honesty, patience, creativity, forgiveness, and resilience.

Through this process of self-reflection, you subjectively

come to know, understand and experience your own *self*, known as your personal identity (Damon & Hart, 1988).

This book will present a proactive therapeutic approach to identifying, developing and expressing your self-concept in the conduct of your personal life, relationships and career, called "Conscious Therapy." This seven-step experiential, gestalt system is designed to give you insight into the dimensions, components, and layers of *self* through experiential self-awareness techniques, and to learn to express your emerging *self* as you deal with the challenges of anxiety, depression and loneliness.

Conscious Therapy will free you from what Lamden (2006), calls negative "life-scripts," and to replace them with a more realistic and positive self-concept. Conscious Therapy is a new gestalt developed by the authors, through our clinical experience, which can be used as a self-help approach by lay-persons, as well as by psychotherapists and psychiatrists, as a new therapeutic approach.

Emler (2002) posits that the development of the self-concept begins in childhood, based on the child's interpretations of interactions with primary caregivers. Lieberman (2008) suggests that children tend to interpret negative interactions with caregivers as being the result of flaws within themselves. For example, a child whose mother is critically ill, and therefore unable to care for her, may conclude, based on her experience, that she is "unlovable" or otherwise defective. This perception becomes integrated within the child's subconscious mind as her "identity" and will likely shape and motivate her decision-making later in life. This is what is meant when we psychologists suggest that a child's personality is basically set by the time she is five years old. (Nave, et al., 2010)

A child under the age of five does not have the ability to self-reflect (Tracy & Robins, 2009) because his ability to evaluate feedback from his environment about his self-concept is not yet developed. This, coupled with the fact that the child's ability to cope with emotional pain is limited may cause a child to develop a negative self-concept when he encounters more distress than he can handle (Lieberman, 2008). Whereas well-adjusted adults have the ability to integrate hurt feelings into their overall self-concept, (Lieberman, 2008), children tend to absorb emotional pain, allowing it to remain stuck in their body-mind, which manifests as negative self-assessments, self-defeating defense mechanisms, and crippling anxiety (Lamden, 2006).

Lamden (2006) finds that you can rise above the faulty self-concepts that you may have developed in childhood, by releasing stuck feelings and by discarding negative self-assessments. In addition to this process of identifying and healing emotional wounds, you must take responsibility for developing and asserting a positive self-concept in the present, so that you can replace an unhealthy way of operating in the world with a healthy internal operating system characterized by emotional independence.

With a healthy, independent sense of self, you can learn to engage in relationships with confidence and resilience. In addition, a strong self-concept allows you to cope with occupational setbacks, romantic break-ups, and the death of loved ones. (Zeiger-Hill, Holden, et. al., 2016). Conscious Therapy is tailor-made to help you do just that.

A Brief History of Self Theory

Self-concept is defined as the "self" or identity, namely, a consciousness and awareness of a person's "I," who possesses body and mind, known as the "me," and whose "I" can effect changes in both the body and the mind. (Spero, 2004). When the "I" becomes aware of the various drives and aspects of the "me," it gains an awareness of its own personality, and then can become accountable for its actions.

Plato posited an early self theory suggesting that a person has:

Appetites—needs and desires;

Reason—the logic of the mind; and

Spirit—emotion and self-assertion.

Plato's self theory states that man must organize his self such that Reason controls both his Spirit and Appetites. (Spero, 2004).

Two thousand years after Plato, Freud developed a strikingly similar self-theory, based on three major structural systems:

Id—instinctual drives;

Ego—the world outside the self;

Superego—the conscience and social norms developed during childhood.

The commonality between Plato and Freud is that they both identified a self comprised of:

Appetites, Id—natural instinct and drives that power and motivate the self;

Reason, Ego—the "I" of the self; the decision making center where Free Will resides;

Super-Ego—the "ought" component which supplies the self with goals and navigates the self with don'ts; (Spero, 2004)

William James (James, 1897) identified three elements of the self, as three departments of the mind:

1. Feelings and Emotions; which are similar to Plato and Freud's Appetites and Id;

2. Reason, Willing—the expression of the "I"; similar to Plato and Freud's Reason and Ego;

3. Conceiving, Super-Ego; which is similar to Plato and Freud's Spirit and Super-Ego. (James, 1897).

In ancient classical Jewish philosophy, outlined in the Talmud

(Tractate Brachot 61a-b) we find a similar formulation, as follows:

> Natural Inclination—(called *Yetzer Hara*) similar to Plato and Freud's Appetites and Id; and James' Feelings and Emotions;
>
> Good Inclination—(called *Yetzer Hatov*) similar to Plato and Freud's Reason and Ego; and James' Reason and Willing:
>
> Soul—Free Will, which is expressed through the Life Force (called *Neshama*) similar to Plato and Freud's Spirit and Super Ego; and James' Conceiving.

The classical Jewish view of a healthy self-concept is that every person is born with a pure God-Given "self" at birth, and must develop that self through the exercise of his Free Will, which is essentially an extension of his Godliness. This "I"/"self" is essentially the conscious self which has to choose between the instincts and drives of his Appetites/Id/Natural Inclination, and the Conscience and Positive Inclinations of his Spirit, Super-Ego/Conceiving Self, in order to make positive moral choices. Due to criticism and challenges to a child's emerging self, the child can be persuaded by his natural inclination that he is "not good enough."

William James (1897) defines two dimensions of self-hood: The "I" and the "me," which indicate how well a person understands himself. The "me" is comprised of:

1. Body;

2. Social relationships, social roles and personality;

3. Spirituality—intellect and thoughts.

The "I" is comprised of four elements:

1. Agency—the active element of all consciousness;

2. Continuity of the self over time;

3. Distinctiveness;

4. Reflection.

By agency, we are referring to volition and Free Will. Under the rubric of the "I," the "I" can decide to go against the predictability of the physical, social, and psychological dimensions of the self. This points to the locus of control that the "I" has, as opposed to the "me." Mead (1934) states that self-knowledge occurs when the "I" gains awareness of the "I" and the "me."

Based on our brief overview of the self theories of Plato, Freud, James, and classical Jewish thought, we posit that the human psyche is comprised of three basic components:

1. Physical or behavioral self—based on Appetites/ Id/Me/Natural Inclination

2. Emotional self—based on Reason/Ego/Willing/ Positive Inclination

3. Cognitive or soul-self, based on the Spirit, Super-Ego/Conceiving/I/Free Will.

The goal of Conscious Therapy is to use seven experiential techniques to help you develop and experience an understanding of your self-concept at these three levels of consciousness. Conscious Therapy addresses the "I" and the "me" awareness of self—and helps this conscious self develop a healthy self-concept and restores your ability to make healthy life choices from a perspective of self-worth and self-efficacy.

THREE

CONSCIOUS THERAPY: STEP ONE
The Wheel of Strengths-
The Cognitive Self

S tep One of Conscious Therapy focuses on the self-concept at the cognitive level. Conscious Therapy posits that having an intellectual awareness of your abilities and strengths stands at the core of your ongoing responsibility to develop a healthy self-concept. If you do not realize who you are, namely, if you do not know which of your character traits give you intrinsic value and self efficacy, you will not be able to actualize your potential, nor make your unique contribution to society (Rabbeinu Yonah of Gerondi, known as Rabbeinu Yonah, circa 1250 CE).

The first step of Conscious Therapy is to complete the "Wheel of Strengths" (seen to the right) to help you develop a working knowledge of your intrinsic worth and competence.

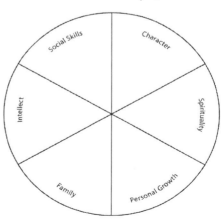

The Wheel of Strengths comprises six dimensions of the "self": intellectual abilities, social skills, character traits, morality and spirituality, contribution to family, and personal growth. Indeed, developing an awareness of your strengths is a dynamic and lifelong endeavor. This exercise will make you aware that you have the ability to apply your strengths to life's challenges.

Complete the Wheel of Strengths by writing two positive strengths you have in each category. Here are some questions to help you complete the Wheel of Strengths:

INTELLECT: Did you act in a street smart manner today? How did you use your common sense today? How did you problem-solve today? Are you book smart/academic? Are you quick witted? Do you have a sense of humor? How did you get organized today?

SOCIAL SKILLS: How did you show empathy and emotional support to someone today? How did you show friendship today? Are you a good listener? Can you keep a confidence? Are you helpful to those in need? Are you involved in the community? Are you dependable and reliable? Do you encourage others? Do you build people up when they are down? Are you reassuring? Loyal? Committed? Loving? Sharing? Tolerant? Understanding? Would you help a friend change a flat tire at three in the morning in the rain?

CHARACTER: Which of the following character traits did you use today: affectionate, compassionate, considerate, appreciative, gracious, giving, patient, truthful, honest, integrity, creative, forgiving, calm, gutsy, disciplined, persistent, think positive, resilient, sensitive, spontaneous, visionary, ambitious, driven…? Which of these character traits are the ongoing theme of your personality? These traits help you discover the "stuff" you are made of, and who you are, in your essence and core self.

SPIRITUALITY: How did you act inspired and energized today? Do you reflect on the meaning of life or on how to improve yourself? Are you moved by nature hikes, waterfalls and sunsets? Do you see a guiding hand in your life? Do you believe in a Higher Power? Do you know how to access your Higher Power? Do you dialogue with your Higher Power? Do you enjoy doing acts of kindness for others? What energizes you?

FAMILY: What did you do today to show love to a family member? Did you show respect today to a member of your family? What do you bring to the table today in your relationship with your spouse/significant other? Do you encourage your family? Does your family encourage you? Do you encourage independent thinking in your family? Are you loved? Do you give love?

PERSONAL GROWTH: What did you do today to go beyond your comfort zone? What are you working on in terms of self-improvement? How have you grown in character and self-discipline over the past year? In what way to you feel accomplished today?

Use this Wheel of Strengths as an ongoing homework assignment. Place a copy of your Wheel of Strengths in key locations: on your refrigerator, your night table, and next to your computer. Noticing the Wheel of Strengths will present you with ongoing opportunities to become conscious of your strengths and values, and to practically employ them in the areas in which your "self" interacts with your environment. At the end of each day, record in a notebook or journal the significant contributions that you made that day in each of the six areas of the Wheel of Strengths, and record any new strength that did not occur to you previously. For example, write the date in your journal and list the six categories of the Wheel of Strengths. Next to "Intellect" you might write that you problem-solved and came up with an innovative solution at work. Next to the "Character" section record how you used your attribute of compassion and provided emotional support for a colleague at work.

After two weeks of completing this assignment, you will have not only familiarized yourself with your positive qualities, you will have trained yourself to view each day as an opportunity to express your unique combination of personal attributes, effect positive change on your environment, and make an effective contribution to others. After two weeks reflect upon your journal entries, which will create a sense of self-awareness and the beginning of consciousness.

While it is important to identify and record your strengths in all six areas of the Wheel of Strengths, it is the category known as "Character" that is most critical to the goal of achieving consciousness. Character traits may include perseverance, leadership, inner strength, compassion, empathy, kindness, honesty/truthfulness, creativity, forgiveness, resilience, affectionate, considerate, appreciative, gracious, giving, patient, integrity, calm, gutsy, disciplined, persistent, think positive, resilient, sensitive, spontaneous, visionary, ambitious, driven. Your character strengths are the key to Conscious Therapy and will be developed in the next steps of Conscious Therapy.

CONSCIOUS THERAPY: STEP TWO
Soul State–
The Emotional Self

Step Two of Conscious Therapy helps develop the emotional component of your self-concept. The emotional self is the bridge between the cognitive self (Step One of Conscious Therapy), and the physical self (Step Three of Conscious Therapy). If the "I" of self reacts to life challenges with fear or anger, and without awareness of its own power of volition, or Free Will, you will automatically descend into the reactive, physical self. If you are insulted, for example, you might instinctively respond with a counter-attack, insult, shouting, or social withdrawal. Your lack of control over your emotions will cause you to respond from your physical self, referred to by William James, 1897, as the "me," by Plato as the instinct, by Freud as the Id, and by Jewish thought as the natural inclination.

If however, you gain insight and awareness of a wider range of the self, namely your "I", then you could learn to respond to emotional distress with a consciousness of your own volition, agency, and Free Will. You can then choose to transcend the hurt feelings of the me/body/id/natural inclination. You can then respond to the presenting challenge from a place of conscious intellect, thus operating from your "I."

This second step of Conscious Therapy will empower you to respond to emotional challenges from your conscious self rather than resorting to an instinctive, visceral, impulsive reaction.

The Soul State exercise begins with a relaxation technique which quiets the mind, and allows you to become conscious of and comfortable with, your feelings. This is achieved through progressive muscle relaxation and diaphragmatic breathing. The muscles relax on the exhale, as you progressively tense and then relax the muscles of your brain, eyes, cheeks, jaw, neck, back, arms, and legs.

Once you have relaxed these muscle groups, imagine an inspiring landscape or place that you have actually visited and which you find relaxing and rejuvenating. It may be the Grand Canyon, a mountain, lake, or sunset. In your mind, go to that inspiring place and notice the landscape with all its colors, sounds, warmth, and scents. Feel the place. Experience the sense of calm and relaxation that you feel when using your imagination to revisit this place. Once you are calmly experiencing this landscape, now realize that the reason this place of external beauty brings you to a state of inner calm is because it reflects the Grand Canyon, mountain, lake, or sunset that resides within your inner self. Delve deeply into your inner self and find the warmest, most sensitive and relaxed part of yourself. That is the Grand Canyon, mountain, lake, or sunset within you. This sense of peace within your psyche arises because this place inside you represents—and symbolizes—your best attribute, discovered in the Character section of your Wheel of Strengths, referred to on pages 28-30, above. Your "I" or core self is drawn to the Grand Canyon, mountain, lake, or sunset because it senses a similarity and affinity with the meaning and spiritual-ity of that place. In other words, your inner awareness and inner consciousness intuits and "sees" itself in this inspiring place. This is why you feel so wholesome, uplifted, liberated, and energized when imagining and revisiting that place.

If you are a visual person and the beautiful place that you imagine is a lake, ocean, or waterfall, then your "I" is intuiting or seeing itself as flowing, giving, sensitive, nurturing, or creative. Since water flows and gives, then you are intuiting your own giv-ing, nurturing and sensitive nature symbolized by the water, lake, ocean waves or waterfall. If your soul state is a canyon, mountain range, landscape, or sunset, then your inner "I" is intuiting itself as strong, powerful, visionary, or creative. In that case you likely possess a strong will or a sense of conviction, as a mountain rep-resents power and strength. Your core self senses a kindred spirit with the visual image that inspires you, and this resonates with your emotional self. Your conscious self is beginning to stir.

Your inner consciousness connects with this "beautiful place" because there is a correlation between your best character trait and the spiritual energy that this place in nature represents. You feel calm and expansive when you experience being in this inspiring place because it mirrors your own beautiful place, your best attri-bute that resides within your psyche. When you contemplate and introspect on this place in nature, it mirrors an awareness of the place within your psyche where the attribute resides; the result is a feeling of wholesomeness, contentment and inner alignment.

If you are not a visual learner, what may work is to bring to mind a certain event or experience from your past that brought you to a state of wholesomeness, calm, relaxation and inspiration by evoking a recollection of personal success, or accomplishment that you felt at that time. For example, you may recall your graduation, the birth of a child, or overcoming a difficult challenge. Go to the memory of that moment of accomplishment and re-experience it in the her and now. This experience will place you in soul state—and you will experience a sense of inner inspiration, motivation and empowerment. You will feel "alive" and energized.

If you practice going to Soul State when you are not under stress or duress, you will then be able to your Soul State equanimity even when you find the world around you is challenging. You can then re-experience the feeling of accomplishment that you felt at the moment of success. For example, if the accomplishment occurred through kindness, then your core self has an affinity toward kindness, sensitivity and nurturing. If the moment of accomplishment occurred through strong will or perseverance, then your core self will likely be one of conviction, strong will or leadership.

In order to experience the serenity and empowerment that comes with being connected with your highest attribute, Conscious Therapy homework suggests that you visit your inspiring place or inspiring moment several times a day, for thirty seconds at a time, until you can call upon and experience your Soul State at will.

The Soul State can be used to center or ground yourself when events around you are causing you upset or inner turmoil. Then you can interact with the environment from your Soul State—as that allows you to access your conscious identity—your true self—hence the term Conscious Therapy. You can "go to" your Soul State and deal with the presenting challenge from your true self, i.e. giving, nurturing, compassionate, strong will, truthful. When you practice this technique you will have learned a new coping mechanism by operating from your conscious self.

CONSCIOUS THERAPY: STEP THREE
The Circle of Control–
The Behavioral Self

S tep Three of Conscious Therapy, allows the "I" to become aware of the "me" in the physical or behavioral
sense (James, 1897; Meade, 1934). In this Step Three, Activating the Behavioral Self, Conscious Therapy encourage
syou to take your physical health seriously. Maintaining a
healthy diet, getting enough sleep, and engaging in regular
exercise contribute to the healthy functioning of the "me."

In this Step Three, we present a diagram known as the
Circle of Control. When you focus on factors which are
outside your Circle of Control (e.g., other people's actions,
words, feelings, thoughts, as well as external events like the
weather and acts of terrorism) you becomes anxious because
you are helpless to control these aspects of your life. The
more you worry about the things outside of your control,
the more frustrated and anxious you will become.

Here is the Circle of Control diagram:

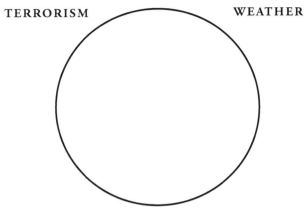

TERRORISM

WEATHER

OTHER PEOPLE'S WORDS, ACTIONS, THOUGHTS, FEELINGS

It is only when you focus on that which is inside your Circle of Control (e.g. your own actions, words, thoughts, and feelings) will you gain a consciousness of your volition, agency and Free Will, namely your "I." When this happens, frustration and anxiety dissipate as you will be consciously focusing on those aspects of your life where you can exercise control and effect change, as follows:

MY:
WORDS
ACTIONS
THOUGHTS
FEELINGS

When you focus on future outcomes, or ruminate over past mistakes, you will likely become anxious. That is because you cannot exert volition, agency or Free Will over the future, or the past. You cannot express your Free Will, or make decisions in the past or future. It is a cognitive distortion to worry about the future, or to agonize over past mistakes. You have no control over the future, and the past is behind you. Psychological health occurs when you decide to cope responsibly with your challenges in the present. This is a matter of mind control, whereby you gain consciousness that when your mind moves to future or past matters, you do have the power to shift your mind focus to the present.

Now let us moved to an advanced level of Conscious Therapy. When facing a life challenge it will be insightful to combine the behavioral tool of the Circle of Control (Step Three) with the cognitive tool of the Wheel of Strengths (Step One). You will gain greater self-understanding and self-awareness by physically taking the Circle of Control and superimposing it on top of your Wheel of Strengths. By doing so, you becomes conscious of your power to effect change in the present by discerning which strengths and abilities within your Wheel of Strengths toolbox you can bring to bear in order to resolve the presenting challenge. You can address the challenge with volition, agency and Free Will, in the present. You can tangibly see that you can effect change in the present by using your Circle of Control i.e. your actions, and words, because they are based on your actual abilities, which you yourself recorded in your Wheel of Strengths.

~~~~~~~~~

Let us now briefly review the first three steps of Conscious Therapy: Cognitive, Emotional and Behavioral dimensions of self concept. In order to proactively develop your conscious self-concept at the cognitive, emotional, and behavioral levels of self, consider the following stick figure which illustrates the three dimensions of self, as follows:

COGNITIVE: Wheel of Strengths

EMOTIONAL: Soul State

BEHAVIORAL: Circle of Control

When cognitive awareness is aligned with emotional awareness, then the behavioral dimension of self can move the self forward through acts of Free Will. This diagram allows you to understand how the concept of "I" (James, 1897), can move the "me," forward with acts of Free Will and volition. The "I" of self is your conscious Free Will; your decision-making center. It is the inner generator which directs your mind, feelings and actions. The "me" of self are the mind, feelings and behaviors that make up your body-mind.

While the first three steps of Conscious Therapy teach you to proactively fashion a conscious self-concept at the cognitive, emotional, and behavioral levels of the psyche, you must now learn to protect this new sense of self from negative self-talk and unresolved emotional pain. To deal with this reality, Conscious Therapy posits that you must now develop the defensive apparatus necessary to respond to emotional and cognitive assaults on the conscious self-concept, and this is indeed the purpose of the fourth, fifth, and sixth steps of Conscious Therapy.

SIX

CONSCIOUS THERAPY: STEP FOUR
The Thought Highway

The Fourth Step of Conscious Therapy, the "Thought Highway," teaches you to cope with negative self-talk and your inner critical voice. Although automatic thoughts may seem real, they are merely electrical impulses in the brain and have no real substance. These automatic thoughts tend to challenge and contradict the positive cognitive, emotional and behavioral "self" that you developed in Steps One, Two and Three, of Conscious Therapy.

Some examples of critical, automatic thoughts are:

"You failed again, you loser."

"You will never amount to anything."

"You are in over your head."

"You are going to lose this relationship."

"This is too much."

Conscious Therapy posits that the key to coping with negative thoughts is to become aware of them and to use a mindfulness technique to watch them pass through your mind. To illustrate this point, let us introduce the tool known as the Thought Highway, a diagram of a freeway depicting happy thoughts as cars, and negative thoughts as large trucks. Imagine a negative thought of worry, and dispassionately watch it drive by, as if watching an eighteen-wheel truck rumble down the highway until it disappears from sight. As the truck, which represents the negative thought, disappears from sight and mind, in that moment, you will return to equanimity. When the negative thoughts pass by, and clear your mental field, you are restored to your conscious self, acquired through utilizing the techniques of the Wheel of Strengths, Soul State and the Circle of Control. When you reset yourself through the use of your Wheel of Strengths, Soul State and Circle of Control, you will revert to positive cognitions, until the challenge of coping with your automatic, rumbling, negative "truck" thoughts inevitably starts all over again. Even though negative thoughts will keep coming throughout the day, you can place the negative thoughts on the Thought Highway and imagine the thoughts passing by. Once the thought clears the mind, you can restore your default healthy self-concept—by using the techniques of the Wheel of Strengths, Soul State and Circle of Control.

You have now reset yourself and have regained the opportunity to make Free Will decisions from a state of full consciousness.

SEVEN

CONSCIOUS THERAPY: STEP FIVE
Creating a Positive Mantra

While the Thought Highway enables you to deal with the automatic thoughts which typically accompany anxiety-provoking situations (e.g., "my mother-in-law is coming for the weekend"), many anxiety attacks go much deeper, and come from learned patterns of thinking or from the subconscious mind. Accordingly, in this Fifth Step of Conscious Therapy, you will learn to create a positive mantra. Your positive mantra or "self-talk" will challenge and replace cognitive distortions, i.e. "I am a failure," "I am no good at relationships." You will learn to reset yourself from the emotional distress that arises from the cognitive distortion, with mantras like, "Life is tough—but I am tougher," and, "I am learning to communicate my needs and stand up for myself."

The key to overcoming the attacks of your critical inner voice is to utilize a Cognitive Behavioral Therapy technique which is based on the fact that your thinking has a direct impact on the quality of your mood. Positive mantras will replace the faulty and inaccurate beliefs that you subconsciously maintain about yourself.

Burns (1999) identified several cognitive distortions or thinking errors that typically lead to emotional distress. Eight of the most common distortions are:

1. All or Nothing Thinking. i.e. *I am a failure.* This is a distortion because life is not black and white and there is no such thing as being a failure all the time.

2. Overgeneralization: This is a distortion because something that happened in one situation will not necessarily happen in all situations.

3. Maximizing Negatives: When you are thinking negatively you tend to become fixated on the negative aspects of the situation which is a distorted view of reality.

4. Minimizing Positives: When you are thinking negatively you tend to minimize and discount the positive aspects of a situation. This is not thinking straight.

5. Fortune Telling: It is a cognitive distortion to "foresee" the future and predict failure and negative outcomes. This is a distortion as you can just as easily train yourself to predict positive outcomes. After all, you are not a prophet.

6. Labeling: Referring to yourself as a "loser" or a failure is a distortion. People are not labels. You may have had a setback and may have failed at a particular project but you are not a failure. You may have made a mistake, but you, yourself, are not a mistake.

7. Should Have...Could Have...Would Have...

These are examples of fantasy thinking that things *Shoulda, Woulda, Coulda* ... been better, if only...This is not thinking in reality, but in fantasy. You are not prepared to deal with the reality of the situation and it is a distortion to avoid reality.

8. Blaming others or self-blame: These are cognitive distortions because they fail to deal with the issues that you are currently facing. They fail to put you in a frame of mind to marshal your strengths and resources to deal with and cope with the reality at hand.

As a general rule, cognitive distortions lead to self-criticism. To the extent that they propel you into an emotional tailspin over past events or catastrophic fears about the future, they are harmful to maintaining a positive self-concept. The Wheel of Strengths, Soul State and the Circle Control, on the other hand, empower you to think positively about yourself, and to focus on the only thing over which you truly have control: your conduct in the present. As such, you must replace the cognitive distortions with a positive mantra that you can use many times a day to keep yourself aligned with your Conscious Self. Positive mantras can include:

"Things are challenging but I can handle this."

"This is hard, stay focused."

"I have been there before, and I will overcome this."

"I can bounce back."

"Let's look at the big picture."

"I've got this."

EIGHT

CONSCIOUS THERAPY: STEP SIX
The Inner Child

The Sixth step of Conscious Therapy, known as the "Inner Child," enables you to deal with unresolved emotional wounds from childhood. For example, a child whose father is consistently belittling him may come to believe that he is defective, unlovable, or simply "not good enough." Over time, children living with relentless criticism and judgment may begin to internalize their emotional wounds and develop a negative self-assessment.

The Inner Child technique, designed to help you heal your wounded Inner Child, has two aspects. First, you must honor and feel the emotional pain of your Inner Child. Your Inner Child's grief, anger, and shame must be permitted to be experienced, for in doing so, you honor and validate your Inner Child, allowing the Inner Child the acknowledgment, attention and respect that she lacked in childhood. Second, the Inner Child must be given the nurturing and support that she needs to confront her pain, which she will get from your Conscious Self.

The way to access your Inner Child is by first bringing to mind the Conscious Self that you have fashioned using the first three steps of Conscious Therapy, and have your Conscious Self serve as an Inner Parent to comfort and heal your own wounded Inner Child. The way to do this is to look at your Wheel of Strengths, which represents your Inner Parent, and imagine you are traveling back in time to "meet" your Inner Child at a time when your Inner Child experienced an embarrassing or traumatic event. When your Inner Parent imagines and experiences the pain of her Inner Child, and "finds" the Inner Child as a younger version of yourself, in his bedroom, school or other situation, have your Inner Parent express to your Inner Child a unique message of encouragement and love. The goal is that instead of the Inner Child holding the Adult Self emotionally enslaved to the pain of the past, the Inner Parent goes "back in time" to the Inner Child and encourages the child to join your Inner Parent, in the present.

It is difficult let go of the pained self-concept that you acquired during childhood. Your Inner Child, even though it is in pain, is a familiar version of yourself, and gives you an identity, albeit a negative one. However, be aware and conscious of the fact that you possess an earlier identity which pre-dates the painful events and the self-defeating subconscious conclusions that you formed as a child. Your Inner Child was born inherently good and worthy, long before you were emotionally wounded by a dysfunctional or critical upbringing. With this knowledge, your Inner Parent can reprogram your Inner Child, that at her essential core, she is worthy and competent and that she is not the sum total of negative experiences foisted upon her by her adult caregivers.

These negative experiences were foisted upon your Inner Child by significant others upon whom you were then dependent for survival. Your emerging sense of self at that time had no choice but to accept the opinions of the adults in your life, in order to ensure your own survival. Once your Inner Parent understands and empathizes with the emotional pain of your Inner Child, your Inner Child will no longer control the mood and emotions of your Adult Self. Then the Adult Self is set free, and is able to respond appropriately and effectively to the responsibilities and the challenges that you face in the present. This is the moment you gain consciousness and become a Conscious Self.

During this journey back in time to your Inner Child, have your Inner Parent express words of love and support to your wounded Inner Child and tell the child that you are here for her and will always be here for her. Enter into a dialogue with your Inner Child and discover whether there is any resentment on the part of the wounded Inner Child against the Inner Parent for having been neglected, abandoned or rejected by the Inner Parent. The Inner Parent will then "work it out" and come to an emotional understanding or resolution with your Inner Child. It may take a number of sessions to have the Inner Parent visit the various moments of trauma and pain experienced by your Inner Child.

During the exercise, have your Inner Parent take your Inner Child to your own beautiful place identified in Step Two as your Soul State. In this manner your Inner Parent can nurture your Inner Child with an emotionally calming experience. Furthermore, the Inner Parent will thereby introduce your Inner Child to the child's true identity by familiarizing your Inner Child with her highest and best character attribute which is symbolized by the beautiful place found in Soul State, as we described in Step Two of Conscious Therapy. In this way, the Inner Parent can begin the healing process by replacing your Inner Child's faulty subconscious perception of her being abandoned, "bad" or a failure. This can be replaced with a healthy self-concept and the Inner Child's awareness of her true self, i.e. caring, a leader, compassionate, patient, loving, giving, sensitive, truthful, creative, strong-willed, resilient or persevering. By gaining an awareness of her true identity, the Inner Child becomes conscious of her true value and worth.

NINE

CONSCIOUS THERAPY: STEP SEVEN
Choosing Love over Fear

The Seventh and final step of Conscious Therapy, known as "Choosing Love over Fear," asks you to make a Free Will decision to choose your own independent attitude toward life. This proactive conscious choice arises from your newly created identity that has been forged during Conscious Therapy. This would entail choosing self-value and self-love, over feelings of self-loathing and perceptions of inadequacy. You will choose to see yourself as worthwhile, as opposed to worthless.

All emotions are based upon, and flow out of, two foundations: love—as the foundation of all positive emotions, and fear—the foundation of all negative feelings, as follows:

LOVE	FEAR
Giving	Taking
Happiness	Depression
Compliments	Criticism
Positivity	Negativity
Optimism	Anxiety
Joy	Anger

This Seventh step, Choosing Love over Fear, is based on the previous six steps of Conscious Therapy. When you proactively work through the seven steps of Conscious Therapy, you will have developed the life-skills that create feelings of self-love which will then allow you the emotional space to develop a positive self-concept. For example, you are now consciously aware of your Wheel of Strengths on a cognitive level (Step One). You have gained an emotional consciousness by tapping into your "Soul State" to experience a feeling of positive emotional energy (Step Two). You have also gained the ability to then apply your cognitive and emotional self- awareness on a behavioral level by focusing on the things over which you have control and by taking proactive steps to do that which is in your power to effect change in the present. (Step Three).

In addition to proactively developing and expressing a healthy self-concept, Conscious Therapy has taught you to defend yourself against the cognitive negativity that would seek to undo your self-concept. You have learned to disengage from your automatic thoughts by allowing negative cognitions to pass through your mind via the Thought Highway which keeps your Conscious Self intact. (Step Four). You have learned to utilize a positive mantra by correcting cognitive distortions and using positive self-talk. This keeps the emotional self-concept intact. (Step Five). You have learned to embrace the consciousness of the cognitive/emotional/ behavioral "self" that you developed through Conscious Therapy as your true identity. You can then use this healthy self-concept to heal your wounded Inner Child and thus allow yourself to function in the present without being emotionally sabotaged by the unresolved pain of your Inner Child. (Step Six).

The Seventh Step of Conscious Therapy now asks you to make a choice between living with an attitude of conscious love, or subconscious fear. If you live with anger, negativity and criticism of others, be aware that the underlying cause of this mode of being is subconscious fear. When you get angry or criticize someone, this is as a result of a perceived existential threat to your inner value or sense of worth. If someone insults, criticizes or ignores you, your resultant anger or depression is caused by your feeling undervalued or unrecognized. Your anger or sadness is coming from a a subconscious fear that you are not valued, respected and worthy.

Step Seven of Conscious Therapy invites you to let go of your anger and negativity which is coming from the fear of a lack of existential value. Based on the healthy cognitive/emotional/behavioral "self" that you have developed during the course of Conscious Therapy, you are now conscious of your inner value and worth and you can therefore choose to adopt an attitude of love and positivity. You can now embrace an attitude of self-love based on your newly developed healthy self-concept, and become an effective decision maker.

To do this, your homework is to create and review a daily gratitude list of ten things that you would not want to not live without. When you become consciously aware of the positives in your life, you will be able to choose an attitude that you are actually loved, which will lead to positivity, being complimentary of others, happiness and becoming a proactive giver.

Another homework exercise for Step Seven is to record five things that are going right in your life. Despite life's inevitable difficulties and challenges, you can train yourself to focus on the positive. When you do so, you will give yourself the opportunity of feeling loved, even in challenging times.

When you are conscious you will be able to reflect on the unique contribution that you can make to your family, community or society, based on the strengths of which you have now become consciously aware. From a perspective of a positive self-concept you are encouraged to continue growing and contributing positively to your environment.

Through Conscious Therapy, the conscious self will become aware the three dimensions of self, namely Cognitive, Emotional and Behavioral as depicted by this diagram:

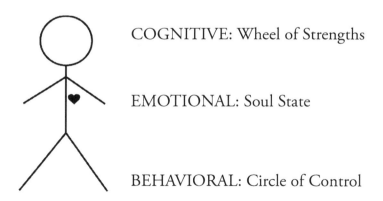

COGNITIVE: Wheel of Strengths

EMOTIONAL: Soul State

BEHAVIORAL: Circle of Control

The Cognitive Self has two parallel sets of thoughts, as follows:

POSITIVE:	NEGATIVE:
I am a giver	I am a taker
I will find ways to make more money	My boss...thinks I am awkward
I am trusted and respected	I have money problems
I am clean and sober	I am too old
I have a family	I am lonely

In using the first step of Conscious Therapy we learn that "thoughts are just thoughts." It is our Conscious Self which decided which thoughts to think, integrate and live by. The mind is only a tool of the Conscious Self and instead of letting my mind control "me", I use my Conscious Self to control, direct and channel my mind. My Conscious Self is synonymous with my Free Will to choose to think what "I" want to think. My Free Will requires tremendous willpower to have the "I" or soul, direct, guide and channel the "me" to where the soul wants it to go.

My Emotional Self has two pathways, as follows:

POSITIVE:	NEGATIVE:
Enthusiasm	Resentment
Joy	Fear
Love	Worry
Awe	Self-pity
Humility	I should have
Endeared	Beat myself up
Connected	Withdraw

Through Conscious Therapy, I come to realize that my moods follow my thoughts. Through mind-control and mindfulness, I can go to my Soul State and thereby effectively choose my mood.

On the behavioral level of self I have two options:

POSITIVE:	NEGATIVE:
Self-control	Lack of restraint
Hold my tongue	Sarcasm
Speak respectfully	Criticism
Prayer	Impulsive
Make good choices	Lazy
Be helpful	Detach
Exercise	Cold Shoulder

On the behavioral level I can choose to act negatively or positively. The goal of Conscious Therapy is to become consciously aware of and align my Thoughts, Emotions and Actions to become a tool and instrument of my Conscious Self. Then I can use my Free Will to work toward my goals and to self-actualize.

TEN

A Case Study
in Conscious Therapy

Eric began Conscious Therapy at age twenty-eight following years of depression, low achievement in school and career, and poor relationships with women. Eric saw himself as a "loser," peppering his speech with self-demeaning put-downs and other harsh self-criticism. During the intake assessment Eric reported he would invariably emotionally withdraw and retreat in the face of challenges, and had done so for years. Though he was bright and capable, he had chosen to support himself (and was barely supporting himself) with a job in a fast food facility. Perhaps most distressing to Eric, he had been consistently unsuccessful in romantic relationships, and, as he was approaching the age of thirty, had all but given up hope that he would ever find love.

Because Eric had grown up in a home where his parents raised their voices, criticized him and shamed him for his mistakes, he became extremely fearful and defensive in his interactions with others.

The first goal of Conscious Therapy is empathy and

safety. Once trust was established, I began to encourage Eric
to speak about his earliest experiences. It soon became clear
that Eric had suffered a number of emotional wounds as a
child. Eric's younger brother, Bryan, had a serious medical
condition which required much of their mother's attention
and care. As a youngster, Eric witnessed the extra attention
being showered upon his brother and concluded that his
mother's indifference to him must be due to a personal lack
or flaw within him. In addition, Eric's mother was emotionally unstable due to wounds of her own past, and as a result,
was often distracted, angry, or otherwise inattentive to Eric's
emotional needs.

I pointed out to Eric that in light of his upbringing, he
began to forge a subconscious Inner Child identity of fear
and self-doubt. I asked Eric to record his cognitions about
himself, which he did as follows:

- "My own mother doesn't like me–I must be unlovable,"
- "My needs and preferences don't matter anyway."
- "I am not successful in relationships so it is safer
  to withdraw to avoid getting hurt."

Eric saw his inability to change the painful dynamics in
his family as an indication of his weakness and inadequacy.
"I am powerless," he told himself, slowing sinking into help-
lessness and despair.

As he reached adolescence, Eric opted for social withdrawal and experienced social anxiety as he avoided contact
with girls, eschewed academic challenge and success, and
generally kept to himself. While his social avoidance pre-

dictably kept others away, Eric saw his isolation as proof of something he had long assumed about himself: that he was "unlovable." In addition, Eric's inaction in the face of academic or social challenges further corroborated his belief that he was powerless over his circumstances, as inevitably, his passivity only produced further undesirable results.

Once I understood the basic identity that Eric had created for himself, I began to use the Conscious Therapy system to help Eric replace it with a positive self-concept. I gave Eric an overview of the first three steps of Conscious Therapy, explaining that self-concept is developed at the cognitive, emotional, and behavioral levels. I assigned him the homework of Step One—the "Wheel of Strengths," asking Eric to become aware of his strengths in the six categories of personality—intellect, social skills, character, spirituality, family and personal growth.

In faithfully working on his Wheel of Strengths every day for three weeks, Eric began to realize that despite his feeling that he was defective, he had, in fact, a number of positive qualities, including perceptiveness, a sense of humor, and showing an interest in intellectual growth.

Following his becoming familiar with and mastering the Wheel of Strengths, Eric began to develop a healthier emotional self-concept through Step Two, the Soul State. He identified one of his character attributes as kindness, discovering that beneath his feelings of fear and anger, he was actually kind-hearted. Through guided imagery, he remembered a time when he had purchased a sandwich for a homeless man, another time when he had visited and cheered-up the father of a schoolmate, who was grieving the loss of his son, and yet another episode, as a much younger boy, when he had comforted his brother, Bryan, when he had been socially excluded. I had Eric emotionally revisit and relive these episodes and he began to feel a sense of emotional healing.

Eric also came to realize that he had a creative side which surfaced only when he was playing a role, on stage. He had studied theater in college, was a good singer, actor, director, impersonator, comedian, and writer, and he had provided much entertainment for others over the years. In his personal life, however, Eric did not believe that he was worthy of, or capable of, maintaining successful relationships.

Using Step Two of Conscious Therapy, in Soul-State, Eric chose Acadia National Park as his favorite inspiring place. The water surrounding the islands visible in the guided imagery reminded him of his flowing nature—representing his kindness, while the islands, themselves, including the beaches of Acadia National Park, the rocks, the puffins, and whales, etc. comprised something of an artistic masterpiece, which resonated deeply with Eric's creative personality. Eric crafted a daily activity whereby he would look at a photograph of Acadia National Park each morning, recalling that Acadia represented and symbolized his qualities of kindness and creativity, and experiencing an attendant feeling of emotional positivity.

I then introduced Step Three, the Circle of Control, to develop Eric's self-efficacy at the behavioral level. Eric drew a diagram of the Circle of Control and placed it on his fridge. On the outside of his Circle of Control he recorded things that he could not control: his mother's words of criticism, and the reactions of women he interacted with. He reminded himself that he could only overcome social anxiety by focusing on the center of his Circle of Control: namely, his *own* feelings, thoughts, and behaviors in the present, and not on the things that were outside his Circle of Control.

As he began to develop a healthier self-concept and assert his true identity, Eric reported that thoughts of self-doubt were still attacking him. Eric reported that he secretly longed to hold on to the self-doubt as at least it was familiar, and that it gave him a sense of identity—albeit a negative one. At least he knew who he was, "a social misfit," and that gave him an ironic sense of comfort.

I worked with Eric on Step Four—the Thought Highway. Eric learned to manage his negative thoughts by simply letting them pass through his consciousness. Next, Eric created a positive mantra of Step Five, realizing that by thinking in more balanced and positive terms, he could further change his negative self-concept. After much practice in reworking his thinking, Eric realized a fundamental mistake he had been making for years: he had looked at his shortcomings and labeled himself a "loser" which was a cognitive distortion. Eric subsequently began to talk to himself with much more compassion and created a positive mantra, "I have had a challenging upbringing but I have good values and I can make a contribution with those values."

In Step Six, Eric reworked his relationship with himself at the subconscious level—the level of the Inner Child. Eric allowed himself to grieve the losses he experienced during his childhood. He particularly remembered an incident when he was three, before he was toilet-trained, where his mother changed his dirty diaper and thrust it in his face, saying, "Now, you deal with this!"

Though many tears, Eric began to accept the pain of being emotionally estranged from his mother. He felt the sadness of his emotional isolation; the sorrow of feeling disconnected from his mother, and the profound sense of loss regarding the reality that his mother would not likely change. In addition, Eric allowed himself to feel his deep perception of shame and defectiveness caused by his mother investing the bulk of her time and attention in his brother, Bryan, while neglecting Eric.

After allowing his childhood wounds to come to the surface, Eric, the emerging consciously valuable Eric, began to set things straight for his Inner Child. I helped Eric encounter his Inner Child, and explained to him that while the circumstances he went through were painful and unfair, they did not define him.

Eric's Inner Parent told his Inner Child:

- "You're a good boy."
- "You have wonderful qualities, and I love you very much.
- "Mom could not express her love to you because of her strained relationship with her own mother."
- "Look how brave you are to do the work you need to do to overcome so much emotional pain."
- "Eric, I am with you."

Eric thus allowed his Inner Parent to attend to and begin to heal the unresolved pain of his Inner Child.

I then introduced Step Seven to Eric, whereby I presented

him with two posters, Fear and Love. I asked him to consider the emotional ramifications of living a life of fear, and he said that he was tired of his own lethargy, anxiety and bitterness. Eric said that he was ready for that dreaded concept, called "change," and he was willing to risk choosing a life of love, with the possibilities and opportunities that love engendered. Eric decided to make a conscious choice: he was going to choose to live with an attitude of love. With that choice, Eric became conscious.

At the end of six months of Conscious Therapy, Eric developed a consciousness that he had innate value and competence. Feeling more confident, he entered into a healthy relationship with a young woman. He left his fast food career to enter a Master's Degree program in speech therapy.

ELEVEN

From Unconscious to Conscious

James is a twenty-nine year old African-American male who works in a shipping warehouse. He was overwhelmed with anxiety and felt so badly about himself that he was having thoughts of hurting himself, including suicidal ideation. We discovered, in group therapy, that James was publicly shamed by a teacher in Tenth Grade for having received a failing grade on a chemistry lab. The teacher attempted to use "tough love" by publicly showing the class his careless lab report errors in a so-called effort to motivate him to do better. This incident humiliated James to such an extent that he gave up on his goal of being a medical technician. In addition, he developed severe social anxiety and a fear of engaging in peer relationships.

During group therapy, James realized that the lab report incident engendered in James, feelings of inadequacy and unworthiness. These feelings became so pervasive that they plagued him almost every waking hour with an inner dialogue telling him that others were better than him, and that he was not a good person, or employee. He lost confidence in his ability to succeed at life. He "used to" be successful but the pressure of daily living was "getting to him."

I reviewed James' personality strengths that are outlined in his Wheel of Strengths (Step One). I asked him to focus on these positive strengths and to think positively about himself based on these abilities. I asked him to find within himself the place where his finest, warmest, most caring feelings were centered. This is the core of his Soul State (Step Two). It is amazing how a person can change his mood by consciously thinking positive thoughts. It created within James a mindset through mind-control.

I then asked James to suggest a percentage of the time that he accesses his positive "self" and the numbers varied from 1% to 10% of the day, which means that he feels negatively about himself about 90-99% of the day. I then asked James to place his "negative" thoughts in the empty chair that I placed in front of him—Chair B—and to have his positive self, in Chair A, "talk" to his negative thoughts which were now in Chair B. Whenever James' negative self was about to speak I asked James to get up and sit in Chair B—the Negative Self Chair—and respond to his positive self. So he went back and forth between chairs as his Positive Self and Negative Self entered into a "dialogue" with one another. James's positive self said to his negative self:

"You are getting me down, so please leave me alone."

James's negative self answered:

"No way. I am part of you and I am not leaving".

Positive Self: *But you are not helping me. Why do you insist on criticizing me?*

Negative Self: *I am protecting you.*

Positive Self: *I don't call putting me down to be protection.*

Negative Self: *By criticizing you I am keeping you humble. And besides, you don't want the embarrassment of the lab report story to happen again, do you? I am keeping you safe by making you withdraw. You cannot afford another humiliation like that, agreed?*

Then I came in and helped James construct an argument with his Negative Self.

I instructed him to say to his Negative Self, the following:

Positive Self: *Listen. You are expressing my negative thoughts which come from my Negative Self. And I want to remind you that if you want to criticize me, you have to follow the rules of fair play—unlike the Chemistry teacher in Tenth Grade. So when criticizing me you have to do so in a constructive way which can be heard and accepted by me. And I have news for you: until now, you have NOT been speaking to me in accordance with the rules of fair play. You have been putting me down— and that is not acceptable.*

Negative Self: *Too bad!*

Positive Self: *Wrong again! You are a messenger—a representative—of truth and personal growth. You are not here to destroy me. Either you speak to me in accordance with the rules of justice and fair play or I will have to report you to a Higher Authority.*

Negative Self: *I didn't realize you felt so strongly about this. I thought that since you just took my comments without responding for so long that you liked the way I spoke to you. It is for your own good, you know.*

Positive Self: *That's enough! It is not for my own good. I will not accept this anymore. Do you agree to criticize me with positive language and with constructive encouragement like: You can do this....Just modify your behavior....*

Negative Self: *If you insist.*

Positive Self: *I insist.*

Negative Self: *OK, OK. You don't have to get pushy about it.*

Over the course of a few sessions, James practiced this dialogue with me and then got good at becoming aware of his Negative Self, challenging it and correcting it. He soon began to counteract the perceptions in his mind that his boss and peers were criticizing him. They weren't. He just "heard" their comments as criticism because of the low self-esteem he developed in the Tenth Grade. James has now learned to manage the inner critic in his mind. His internal dialogue is now at a manageable level. James has now gone back to school to become a medical technologist.

It is the challenge and crisis which prompts us to delve deeply within our deepest thoughts and feelings, our inner self, and to connect with our conscious psyche. During this process of self-discovery, you will become conscious of your core self which is hiding under layers of emotional pain from negative childhood and teenage hurts. It is then that you will become conscious of your innate goodness and begin to use the gift of positive speech—with yourself.

Using positive speech begins with the consciousness that you have the power to control the inner language that you use—on yourself. You can access the independent essence of self—your core identity—and begin to evaluate your behavior and deeds objectively. When you gain consciousness, then you will choose to stop using the language that critical parents, teachers, or bullying peers have used towards you—which put-downs and criticisms resonate and play in your mind constantly. When you gain consciousness of your true self, you liberate yourself from enslavement to the criticisms, judgments and negativity that you grew up with. You can independently evaluate those old voices and find the strength to say to them, *I hear you. I recognize where you are coming from. These are biased voices foisted upon me in my youth. These voices are not true. I choose to reject them and create my own identity with my own inner voice.*

The emotional pain of the Inner Child can develop in various ways. It develops in childhood mostly as a result of strained interactions with parents who themselves have low self-esteem, and who parent with heavy-handed discipline, power, control and criticism. This applies also to teachers who use this heavy-handed critical style and also applies to peers who bully others. This constant barrage of negativity from parents, teachers or peers can lead your Inner Child, who suffers incessantly from these overly critical interactions, to develop an impression in her subconscious mind that she is no good, is inadequate and unworthy… otherwise why would those around me be so critical of me? It must be me! And this low self-esteem becomes a mindset which the Inner Child carries with her into adulthood. The feeling of unworthiness and inadequacy becomes your Inner Child's mindset, world-view and identity, which becomes the *unfinished business* of your childhood.

Why does my Inner Child form this impression of himself as being inadequate? Children have no sense of "self." They do not have the capacity to evaluate their unique personalities nor do they have a reflective or introspective sense of "who they are" or what kind of person they are. They lack self-awareness. The only way a child learns about his personality is through interactions with significant others and through feedback from parents, teachers and peers, which are called "reflected appraisals." When we say to a child: "Don't touch that...don't do that.....bad boy... bad Girl...when they do something wrong, and we do that a few times a day for 10 years, the Inner Child will have integrated a sense of "badness" into his psyche.

Even if we don't say "bad boy" or "bad girl," and we merely push our children to behave and "fly right" with comments like:

Tuck in your shirt. Don't be so lazy. Stop being so inconsiderate. You are being mean. If your head wasn't screwed on, it would fall off. Oh, here comes our math genius! Will you clean up your room already...how many times do I have to remind you? Come on lazy bones...get up already....That's selfish!....

...all under the rubric of tough love, discipline and "parenting," the Inner Child is left with the impression that he is not "making it"—he is just "not good enough."

How many of these comments do we direct toward our children per day? Of course they are justified because we have to keep them in line and keep our ship afloat, right? So how many "corrective" comments do we make per day... just to keep our family moving in the right direction, of course? 3? 5? 7? Let's be conservative and say that we make

5 such comments to our kids per day. That would be 35 such comments per week or 1,820 such comments per year, which would amount to 18,200 such comments by the time the child is 10 years old! And I still don't know why my child feels bad about herself and keeps putting herself down....Oh really?

We, as parents, and teachers, need to become aware of the educational and developmental fact that we create a child's sense of self through the words, comments and body language we use when we interact with them. We have that power because developmentally a child does not have a sense of "self" other than the one we give them. For example, if we say to a child: *You are kind, giving, sensitive, caring, conscientious, and responsible...* then the child will say... *"I am? I did not know that about myself. I guess I am...because I trust the significant authority figures in my life to tell me the truth about myself and my world."* We have the power to create a positive self-image or a negative self-concept in our children and students...and we must use that power, wisely.

Another source of low self-esteem in children is the emotional fallout when parents divorce. By and large most children need two loving parents to feel secure and protected. When parents divorce, the child, in many, (not all) cases, may subconsciously blame themselves for the divorce. They might say to themselves, subconsciously, *"My parent's arguments were mostly about me—they disagreed about what was "best" for me all the time. If I was a better boy my parents would not have argued so much. If only I was better girl, my parents would still be married."* This feeling of guilt and self-blame in cases of divorce is evident in children of divorced parents even when the child grows into *adulthood* which surfaces as low level depression and low self-esteem. I have treated many adult clients who blame themselves for their parents' divorce, sometimes, 20-25 years after the divorce.

When these "low self-esteem" kids grow up and get married they carry within their inner psyche, feelings of inadequacy and unworthiness. This is called the "unfinished business" of their childhood. And a negative comment by a spouse may well trigger their underlying low self-esteem and the low self-esteem spouse will respond in anger, pain and hurt. If the spouse felt good about himself then he would use an "I" message and say: *I feel hurt.* But he usually responds with: *Well, look who's talking....well you don't speak nicely to me or my parents...last year you forgot my birthday...*and the negativity escalates into a full-blown argument which has little to do with the original hurtful comment.

And this negativity works both ways. The spouse who responds and escalates the argument may be suffering from low self-esteem and the spouse who utters the negative and critical comments on a consistent basis may well be suffering from low self-esteem, as well. The spouse who is critical of his or her spouse may be covering up her own bad feelings by projecting them onto her spouse. The psychological reason for this is that one only criticizes someone else, if you have that issue yourself. If you don't like your spouse's behavior in a certain area, you probably do the same thing in a different form..and you loathe it so much about yourself that you "see it" in your spouse. This is an illustration of the the well-known psychological phenomenon that "If you criticize another, you reveal yourself."

TWELVE

Alone With Yourself

Rick is a thirty-seven year old male who is an industrious handyman. He grew up as a stable-boy. At the age of 11 he was introduced to marijuana and then to cocaine; by age 15 he was a heroin addict. His father beat and belittled him and threw him out of the house at the age of 16. He learned to survive on the street. He was a scrapper and hard-nosed fighter. He became homeless and slept in a truck in the forest for fifteen years. He survived by doing landscaping, selling goods at markets and hauling. He entered a methadone program and stopped using hard drugs and then graduated from the methadone program and stopped using methadone, however, he still smoked marijuana every day. In his thirties he became extremely anxious and wanted to wean himself from his marijuana addiction but felt he needed the marijuana to calm his anxiety. He felt trapped and began having suicidal thoughts. He spent a week in the psychiatric unit of a local hospital and then was referred to our clinic.

Rick's main emotional challenge is loneliness and feeling "alone against the world." He feels abandoned as if the rest of the world is indifferent to him. This state of aloneness is an existential perception that no-one truly understands what he is going through—and he feels isolated, and emotionally abandoned. Rick allowed those feelings to spiral out of control, and then emotional gravity brought him the emotional pain of abandonment, and rejection. It led to depression and physical illness.

During group therapy I taught Rick to go against the gravity of his emotions by activating his conscious self—and become aware that, of course, he is alone—that is because he is unique—with a unique mission to fulfill. No-one else has Rick's unique constellation of DNA, upbringing, experiences, values and beliefs, (Step One of Conscious Therapy) with which to navigate life. I used the Wheel of Strengths, Step One of Conscious Therapy, page 28. I taught Rick that his particular challenge of abandonment and rejection is meant to bring out a dormant or latent ability from within himself, in order for Rick to make a unique contribution to the world.

Rick learned to strengthen his sense of consciousness by taking initiative instead of being a follower. Rick delved into his own thoughts, psyche, fears, and hopes, and decided that he wanted to learn how to leverage his pain and transform it into his destiny. During Step Two of Conscious Therapy, the Soul State, and working through his pain, Rick decided that in order to have his abusive upbringing and substance abuse make sense to him, he would begin to share his experiences with young people who themselves had been abandoned by their parents and who had to make it alone on the streets. He took a course as a Peer Support Specialist, and began visiting juvenile detention centers and homeless shelters and began talking to street-kids about his experiences and how he had lived a life of drug abuse and how he decided to get off drugs and started taking control of his life. This process was therapeutic for him and in some way, served to redeem him from his pain.

Rick taught the street-kids that they contain within themselves all of the attributes that can make them independent, drug free and productive. He taught them that their inner emotional stability derives from the extent to which they achieve conscious independence—to be their own person. He taught them to be street smart—and to find wisdom through their own personal life experiences. He taught them to transform their aloneness into independence by finding wisdom in their own unique crises. He taught them how to grow from the pain.

Rick taught them that real strength was not dependent on defeating another, because they were bound to find people stronger than themselves. Rather, true strength lies in conquering your own negativity, and thereby your strength is self-contained and lives within you, wherever you go. In this way he taught the street-kids how to uncover their own unique, independent strength.

Rick taught them that true wealth is nothing if your worldly possessions are vulnerable to a thief stealing your possessions at night; rather your true wealth is when you find satisfaction with your own self-worth, and are proud of your accomplishments.

Rick taught them that every individual is unique in his nature and his nurture. There is no one else in the universe, past, present or future, with your unique constellation of DNA, attributes, strengths, intellect, emotions, limitations, flaws, upbringing, hopes and dreams.

In other words, each person has a contribution to make to the development of society which only you can achieve. Each of us is perfectly suited and designed to make that contribution—and your job is to discover your unique qualities—and to make that contribution. At the same time, you are aware that your neighbor and others in the community, too, have their unique contributions to make, and you must learn to respect, value and allow them to make that contribution, without hindrance or jealousy.

Each of us has the potential to discover and to work toward achieving our unique destiny. It is both a privilege and obligation to do so, as there are no rights without obligations. That means that you have innate and intrinsic worth. Your innate worth and value as a unique individual obligate you to seek and find that same intrinsic value in others, and give them respect and validation—especially those closest to you: your spouse, children, and parents.

Your uniqueness can be a double-edged sword. On the one hand, it gives you a sense of self-worth. On the other hand, if you take it too far, you might come to think that the world was created for you alone, and not for anyone else. Your uniqueness must not lead you to self-centeredness, selfishness, or haughtiness; rather it must be used with humility, to make the contribution to the world that you are destined to make.

THIRTEEN

The Art of Being

Shawna is a 32 year old woman with two children, ages 16 and 4. Her mother was a heroin addict. As a teenager Shawna had no-one to look after her and at the age of 16 she left home and became an exotic dancer. She was picked up by a major drug dealer and became his girlfriend. A year later she had a child. As she was abused by him and no longer of use to him, she took refuge in a shelter for battered women and then lived in a series of homeless shelters. She became depressed and a heroin addict. She became a prostitute to finance her drug addiction. She was above average in intelligence and persevered despite her addiction, and graduated high school. She knew she wanted a better life for herself and her children and replaced the heroin with methadone and eventually became clean. After a suicide attempt and a stay in a hospital psychiatric ward, she was referred to our clinic to treat her suicidal ideation and depression.

Anyone who wants to find the light within themselves,

has to first delve into the darkness that lies within their own psyche and subconscious self. Shawna had to explore the emotional pain within herself before she could begin to discover her true identity and value. In the overwhelming darkness of her emotional pain, Shawna felt existentially alone, abandoned, afraid. Shawna explored the pain of suffering abuse, and turning to drugs as an escape from the existential pain. Through the work of Conscious Therapy, Shawna's trauma of abandonment, rejection and loneliness was transformed into a *conscious aloneness*. She developed an inner understanding as to what happened, how it happened and her own role in that process. She began to gain insight into her "self."

Let's go deeper. The pain of Shawna's emotional darkness became the catalyst and cause of her emerging awareness and consciousness. This does not mean that her newly discovered awareness that she was intelligent and her goal of becoming a beautician banished the pain of abuse and darkness; rather the darkness and emotional pain transformed itself into light, itself. The light arises from within our own darkness. We have to go to war against the darkness within ourselves— meaning the loneliness within ourselves can be transformed into aloneness, uniqueness and independence.

Before Shawna could start to take action and take steps to look after herself and her children, she had to learn the art of "Being." This means to develop a consciousness that it is a combination of your strengths, limitations and challenges which make you who you are, and create your sense of "self." Shawna's "self" could then become aware that she is worthy of love, can have a life of meaning, and that she is here in this world to achieve a unique purpose and destiny.

As she worked through the steps of Conscious Therapy, Shawna came to realize that the abuse she suffered shaped her character and brought out values and strengths from within her psyche that she did not even know that she possessed. As a teenage drug addict and prostitute, she learned to survive on the streets. Looking back, during Conscious Therapy, she came to realize that she was resourceful and savvy to have survived on the streets. During Conscious Therapy she re-shaped and refined that view of herself and realized, that in essence, she was creative and that she wanted to open her own beautician business. And she became determined to teach her children how to leave the streets by getting an education.

As she delved into her pain and insecurities she began to discover what she wanted out of life. Her loneliness was transformed into aloneness in that she, alone, realized that she had a singular, independent and unique pathway to travel from victim-hood to contributor.

Joseph B. Soloveichik, in his classic essay, The Lonely Man of Faith, states: The "I" is lonely, experiencing onto-logical incompleteness, because there is no-one who exists like the "I,"…tormented by loneliness and solitude."[3]

It was the abuse itself which caused Shawna to question her own value and worth. During Conscious Therapy she spoke openly about the details of her abuse. Shawna asked herself, *Am I deserving of this? Am I so worthless that I deserve to be abused? Am I merely a vehicle of someone else's whims, moods and desires? Am I merely a tool of my abuser's wants? Am*

---

3 Soloveichik, Joseph B., The Lonely Man of Faith, Doubleday, New York, 1968

I worth anything in my own right?

During the course of six months of group and individual Conscious Therapy, Shawna began to identify the "self" and ego that lay underneath her abused victimized self. Shawna became conscious of her own ego, which is the dimension of self that possesses self-reflection and self-awareness. Shawna became aware of her *child-self*, in relation to her parents; her *spouse-self* in relation to her new boyfriend; and her *mother-self* self in relation to her children.

Shawna began to realize that all of her emotional issues, including sadness, anger, frustration, depression and anxiety stemmed from strained and conflicted relationships with her parents, siblings, abusive, drug-pusher ex-boyfriend, and children.

Through guided meditation and mindfulness, (Soul State, Step Two, and Inner Child, Step Six of Conscious Therapy), Shawna learned to travel within and beyond her pained ego and and discovered that she had an innate, valuable and worthy identity, by discovering her own desires, wants and hopes. She developed a consciousness that she was more than her pain, and that her emerging self could contain, and was "bigger" than the pain itself. She discovered that she had value and her own dreams. It was only because she was willing to confront her feelings of worthlessness, that she learned to challenge that assumption and discovered her own value and worth. She learned to transcend her pain and her lonely self and arrived at her alone and redeemed self. She became conscious.

Shawna learned that the physical and emotional world is the vessel which contains a deeper reality—her conscious self, which seeks the true meaning and purpose of her existence. Shawna's valuable "I" became aware of her pained "me". The debasement of her abuse itself became the catalyst for her to delve within herself and extract an inner spirit and innate goodness. When Shawna used Conscious Therapy to come to terms with her abuse, she created within herself an inner strength which allowed her to emerge from the identity of abuse that was foisted upon her by the abusive will of others.

Shawna's conscious self was built on maintaining awareness of her intrinsic "self" in the face of adversity. When Shawna became conscious of her own Free Will to create her own identity, she was able to disregard concerns as to what others would say, taunt or ridicule her. Shawna learned to be alone and independent of other's opinions. She learned to become whole with herself and found oneness with herself.

FOURTEEN

Self-Mastery

Jesse, 31, is a recovering heroin addict. Her mother is a cocaine addict and Jesse does not know who her father is. At the age of 10 she was forced to find a place to live as her mother was incapable of looking after her and her 2 year old brother. Jesse had no relatives and became a street-child. To find shelter she stole a tent from a local supply store and lived under a bridge for two years with her brother. She became a professional thief and stole food, supplies, blankets, generators and heaters, from local stores. No one suspected her as she would go shopping with her little brother and place diapers on top of the food and shelter items in her shopping basket and would simply walk out of the store. She would drop off her brother at day-care as if her mother sent her to drop him off. After two years living under the bridge, she and her brother entered the foster care system. She is highly intelligent and graduated high school and is completing a business degree at university while on methadone. She came to our clinic to deal with overwhelming anxiety.

Jesse's life-story is as devastating as it is humbling. Jesse's sense of humility required silence, privacy, and self-control. The essence of Jesse's self-mastery was to take care of her brother without gratitude or praise from him, or from her parents. She did what she had to do—she had no choice. Jesse learned to actualize her character through surviving, without fanfare, on the streets. She made survival decisions on her own, alone. No-one else exercised those choices, which were thrust upon her by life circumstances. What can we learn from Jesse's tragic silent heroism?

Sometimes we are called upon to show self-control and restraint in our personal lives by refraining from saying something to a spouse or child which might otherwise hurt them. That requires tremendous self-control—and if we succeed, no-one will ever know of our success. It remains hidden. Sometimes we have the opportunity to self-actualize by acting publicly, and by taking a public stand on an issue that requires great courage. This occurs when we are called upon to speak the truth even at great personal risk.

Each of us has a contribution to make on a private or a public level. Some of our contributions will become known to others and some will remain hidden. For the private deeds you must learn to be satisfied with the inner knowledge that you did the right thing merely because it was the right thing.

Each of us, alone, can and must make our unique contribution to the welfare of others. Instead of feeling lonely in our search for what we can do, we can each transform the search into one of aloneness—an opportunity to embrace a unique contribution to the development of others, while developing our own character. Seeking to make this contribution is by definition "other-centered," instead of ego-centered.

We operate in three dimensions of existence: Place, Time and People. It is your conscious self which recognizes the time and place in which you find yourself. You live in the convergence of these three dimensions. Your conscious self—in this place, at this time—is a convergence of factors that never occurred before, and will never occur again; it is unique in history. If you are to truly live in the moment, and make each moment of life count, you must be conscious and aware of this convergence, by extracting from this moment the full import of that which you are supposed to learn from this moment, in this place, at this time, through your interaction with the other conscious beings whom you encounter here and now. This is called being conscious in each moment.

It is the conscious self which perceives its own destiny. During the process of Conscious Therapy, Jesse became conscious of her destiny—to emerge from a sense of abandonment, and to save herself and her brother. In order to achieve this destiny, she marshaled all of her physical abilities and resources in order to achieve that goal. Consciousness means that you are aware that you are traveling toward a destination—which is to be the best person you can become. Your "destination" is much more significant than a particular place; it is the accomplishment of developing your character. Your destiny becomes your destination.

In order to overcome the obstacles and challenges which get in the way of Jesse becoming the best she could be, she had to decide which worldview she wanted to adopt. She could have chosen to be bitter and angry about being brought up by an irresponsible addict who abandoned her; or she could have chosen, as she did, to emerge from that trauma and decide to survive, educate herself, and seek a productive life. When Jesse accessed her power of choice through the exercise of her Free Will, she was, of necessity, alone. Jesse comprises and represents a unique and distinct dimension of Free Will which is alone, unique, and therefore, purposeful. No-one else in the world ever had Jesse's DNA, upbringing—or lack thereof, background, and life circumstances. In other words, her nature and nurture, are unique in world history (Wheel of Strengths, Step One, and Soul State, Step Two, and Positive Mantra, Step Five of Conscious Therapy).Therefore, all of Jesse's decisions, of necessity were, and are, made by her alone. This could have given rise to her feeling abandoned and lonely, but it did not. Through Conscious Therapy she gained an existential awareness of being uniquely primed to do something that no-one else has ever done, with her unique nature and nurture. This awareness, and being in a position to choose which life approach to take, is called consciousness.

> *Richard is 32, and is an accomplished motivational speaker. He majored in theater in college, has an MBA from Columbia, and is an entrepreneur. He is creative and motivates people to succeed in life. Richard has a good friend from college named Zack, who is also very talented. They used to compete with each other for grades and in sports activities. Zack earned a law degree from Yale and is an up-and-coming star lawyer. Richard, is deeply jealous of Zack's success. Zack is now a partner in a Wall Street law firm, does international*

legal mediations and lectures around the world in his
field. He is becoming more well-known than Richard,
and makes more money.

Richard understands, and lives with purpose and destiny—
to be a successful motivational speaker to help people get ahead
and move forward with their lives. If Richard was able to fully
accept and embrace his destiny from a position of true consciousness, then he would not be drawn after the distractions of
jealousy, anger and conceit. For Richard to become conscious
and find the will to achieve his destiny, he would have to gain
a laser-beam focus on his own capabilities and contribution,
without being distracted by Zack's successes. If Richard was
able to see and accept that Zack has his own destiny, and that
each of them is unique and has his own unique contribution to
make, then Richard would free up mind-space that is currently
occupied by jealousy, and use that mind-space to be more creative and productive in his own field. However, since Richard
is not yet fully conscious of who he is, he is allowing external
forces to throw him off track from achieving his unique destiny.

What is destiny? Destiny is the opposite of distraction.
Richard is distracted because he is seeking the feeling of
inner satisfaction that he is more successful than Zack.
Richard lacks wholeness with his own self, perhaps due to
the constant criticism and judgment that he suffered at the
hands of his father when he was growing up. Richard is still
seeking his father's approval and subconsciously feels that if
he is more successful than Zack, then his father will finally
approve of him.

Richard is missing self-acceptance, which leads him to
lack full consciousness. Richard lacks a full mind of his

own; rather his mind is influenced and guided by the will of others, namely his father's opinion of him.

A man of distraction is shaped by men of destiny. Richard's jealousy causes him to lack consciousness, and he therefore ceases to have his own Free Will. Instead of being an independent thinker, Richard becomes a slave to his need for acceptance. If Richard gained consciousness, he would focus and embrace his own destiny, without being distracted by Zack and the need for his father's approval. He would be liberated from the "need" for validation from others, and his Will would be Free. Without full consciousness Richard does not have Free Will. His Will is dependent on the Free Will of his father.

FIFTEEN

Depression

Rainelle, aged 35, was sexually abused by her mother's boyfriend when she was 8 years old. The abuse continued for 2 years. One day she overheard her mother tell someone that if anyone ever touched or hurt her child she would kill that person. Rainelle, at age 9, had wanted to tell her mother that she was being molested, but when she heard that her mother would kill her abuser, she was afraid that her mother would go to jail and that she would be left alone to live with the abuser. Rainelle kept silent and held in the pain; and only told her mother about the abuse when Rainelle got married at age 23. Rainelle had three children and ran a successful business. She divorced her husband when she was 35 and when her oldest child was 8, she got depressed. She was able to work and take care of her children but she was not functioning fully. She came to our clinic for help.

Rainelle got depressed because she lost consciousness of her goals. When her oldest child reached the same age she was when she was molested, she began having flashbacks. She kept looking at her child, imagining herself at age 8 and how vulnerable she, herself, had been at that age. She began to relive her abuse. Emotionally, she was stuck at age 8, in place and time, and lost focus on her goal—her destiny.

The way our clinic explored Rainelle's depression was to explain to her that after a person suffers a trauma, when her own child reaches the same age at which Rainelle herself experienced the trauma, Rainelle began to "relive" the unprocessed, unresolved pain of her molestation. Her child achieving the same age that Rainelle was when she abused, triggered Rainelle's painful memories, and she was emotionally frozen in that pain.

We taught Rainelle to liberate herself from that pain by having her identify her Inner Child and having her Inner Parent soothe and calm the inner 8 year old child within her. We also had her identify the part or dimension of her that was abused and had her Inner Parent "talk to" and soothe the pained part of herself. She was able to tell the abused part of her that she had grown up since then and that she had learned skills and had abilities to defend herself now, which she did not have when she was 8 years old. In this way, Rainelle came to realize that her identity was not a "victim of pain." Rather, the pain was only one part of her, and that Rainelle's conscious self was "bigger" than the pain. She learned that her conscious self could contain, respect and accept the pain, and not let the pain control her.

Awareness of Rainelle's adult conscious self brought her to

existential aloneness—and deep inner knowledge of her own "self" and value. Rainelle delved into her inner being and psyche and discovered her innate worth that no-one could damage or harm. This is an inner awareness, consciousness and confidence to travel within, into her subconscious self, to discover her innermost essence—her true identity. This can only be achieved when Rainelle became brave enough to confront the pain of loneliness, abuse and abandonment and allow that part of herself to "die." In fact, when Rainelle was abused, a part of her did "die." Rainelle had to accept the death of this part of her and only then could she start to live again.

It is here that Rainelle encountered her essence by asking herself, "Who am I, really? What is my true nature and how do I define myself? What do I believe and what do I stand for?" For Rainelle to get unstuck from the pain of her past she had to find the emotional fortitude to travel deeper than the pain, and beyond the pain, to the place where no pain exists. When Rainelle looked within her psyche, in a moment of existential consciousness, she came to meet and to know her true self and to discover that it was pure, and untainted. This is a place within the psyche that pre-dates the painful molestation. It is her innate, intrinsic, core self, which no-one can access, except her subconscious self.

When Rainelle delved within herself through deep mindfulness and introspection, she discovered what she truly believed about herself and what she stood for. At that fateful moment, she was existentially alone. In that moment of consciousness, she discovered her "self." That self, that identity, is the core of who Rainelle is. It was the essence of self that was revealed only as a result of her willingness to confront the pain, and go beyond the pain by not allowing the pain that others inflicted upon her, to define her. She would no longer allow the painful actions of her abuser to define her because these actions were not performed by Rainelle's Free Will, rather they were foisted upon her by the Free Will of her abuser. Rainelle learned that only her own Free Will thoughts, feelings and actions could define her. Rainelle thus arrived at a consciousness of self.

SIXTEEN

Assertiveness

Steven grew up in a large family, one of seven children. The house was busy and his parents were hardworking. Steven had to let himself into the house after school every day at 3:30, as his mother was at work and only came home at 5:30 every day. He was a typical latchkey child. Steven had his physical and educational needs met but he never received the touchy-feely warm love that his temperament craved. He went away to boarding school for high school and was typically a quiet and reserved teenager who never got into trouble—and kept to himself. He never got the attention or love that he sought but he did have positive relationships with his teachers and advisors. When Steven married he thought that all would become magically better. His wife was a capable, matter-of-fact woman who was not loving, but assertive. She spoke to him with directness and clarity and expressed that which she needed; she did not show demonstrative love. It was as if Steve married his mother. Steven began to resent his wife and one year old son and did not know why. He felt that his son "gets in my way" and that his wife was just plain "mean." He began to secretly hate his wife and was tormented and felt guilty for harboring those feelings. During Conscious Therapy, Steven came to realize that he had craved love as a child and had hoped that marriage would redeem his emotional loneliness and pain.

In therapy, Steven came to learn that to gain consciousness he had to face his fears and his weaknesses, which could only be done alone. Through deep sessions of mindfulness and meditation, Steven strove to discover why he made the life choices that he did, and what motivated him to marry his wife.

When you set your eyes on an object or a landscape, you see the entire scene at one glance. Your eye grasps and perceives the whole picture as soon as your eye rests on the scene. Hearing, on the other hand, occurs syllable by syllable, until the whole sentence is completed; only then can the listener understand the beginning of the sentence—retroactively, and cumulatively. These are the two ways in which we interact with the world—seeing and hearing. The process of listening and integrating words we hear, and making sense of them, is that which creates a relationship with the person who is speaking with us. The same is true with the process of creating a relationship with your "self." You have to listen to your inner self, syllable by syllable, event by event, inner thought by inner thought, in order to come to understand, retrospectively, after the events of your life have unfolded, what they are "saying" to you, and how the "universe" is prodding you to grow in character.

To survive challenges, you need emotional stamina. It is this inner strength of character which gives you silent, stoic bravery and dignity, in the face of the gravest hardship. This creates an inner strength, born from an inner confidence, to disregard the callous treatment of the world, and find strength in following your inner convictions, irrespective of the cruelty that might be hurled at you. You need a patient confidence in your own inner peace and serenity, that you gain from confronting the formidable challenges of life. Rather than succumb to your afflictions, rather than become a victim to your tormentors, you must stand firm and dignified, feeling consolation in communicating, alone, with your inner destiny. This is how you get to know your "self," and become conscious.

Steven learned that there is a necessity of searing honesty while pursuing the path to self-discovery. He came to realize that he needed love, and that when he entered marriage he was hoping to heal from his feelings of emotional loneliness, through the soft, warm endearing support of his wife. But, that support never came. He had to admit that he was in need of emotional love and acceptance. He had to come to terms with the fact that his upbringing did not lead him to feel worthy of love. This led to Steven's low self esteem, feelings of inadequacy, and a lack of value. He craved love from his wife, and he regretted that he married her.

Tests and challenges in life do not only come in the form of abuse or illness. They can come in the form of a silent, existential loneliness and low self-esteem that can be devastating in causing a quiet depression and dissatisfaction with life. Steven discovered that his redemption was not to change his wife, but to start loving himself. One way he did that was to become assertive and tell his wife what he needed. Another was to become assertive and to respond with his true feelings instead of suffering in silence when he was spoken to aggressively. He began to realize that he was worthy of being spoken to respectfully, and began to speak up for himself. He started feeling better about himself and his resentment against his wife abated.

Steven found the inner voice required to accept his existential loneliness and to transform it into *aloneness*. The concept of *aloneness* means discovering and holding onto his identity—a person who feels worthy of giving and receiving love. He learned to forge and stand up for his identity and thereby started to live consciously by living in accordance with his emerging identity.

When Steven now says ,"I am alone," he means that he has chosen a life mission which is his identity. Once he discovered his sense of self, or consciousness, he began to feel whole. During Conscious Therapy, Steven said, "I realize now that I am free to choose my own, unique, and "alone" identity. True, we are alone on our life journey—but it must be that way. It is out of a sense of obligation that we must exercise our Free Will to formulate our own unique sense of self—and identity, which enables successful relationships.

SEVENTEEN

Bereavement

Mike is 54 and grew up with a childhood friend, Mark, in California. After high school they both enlisted in the US Army and were deployed to Iraq at the same time, in different units. When they were discharged they came back to California and opened a restaurant together. It failed, and they went on to run various other businesses, one of which succeeded. At the age of 53, Mark developed cancer and was told that he had four months left to live. Mike hardly had time to say goodbye to his lifelong friend and he was devastated. It has been two years now and Mike has not been able to shake his depression.

A person who finds himself alone at the loss of a loved one—a parent, spouse, partner, teacher, or close friend, may feel so bereft, despairing and alone, that he will wonder how he can survive without his guide, mentor, and main support. His world has been shattered because his status quo has been shaken. How can he move forward?

He can take comfort in the consciousness that he has the teachings, values, and lifelong guidance imparted to him by his parent, teacher, mentor, or friend, and he can live by those values—and move on. If he settles, calms, and composes himself, he can gain a consciousness and awareness that he does, in fact, have a lifetime of his parent, mentor or friend's guidance integrated within his psyche and therefore, in that sense, he still has the departed person "with him," and he is not alone. He can dedicate his activities and projects to the memory of his loved one. He can keep her memory alive by continuing to live by the values and by applying the values of the person he lost, in his own life.

On a personal note, in 1988, my wife lost her brother, Dovid Brown, z'l, when he was 20. He had been attending Ner Israel Rabbinical College in Baltimore, and died on a Jewish holiday, Purim, in a car accident. He was a very talented young man, learned, motivated, proactive and a giver. He was good at everything he tried.

It was a huge loss for my in-laws, and for all of us. My wife was devastated, and talks of her brother often. When she was asked by another family who had a lost a son, how she coped, she answered that she focuses on the good memories and positive experiences that she did have with her brother, and not on that which she did not have.

My wife chooses to focus on the positive experiences with her brother, his good character, the memories, the good times together, the life lessons he taught her, and all the experiences which made up their relationship. She does not focus on "what could have been," or "what would have been." That would be dwelling on "could have, should have, or would have." That would be the world of fantasy—because what could have been, does not exist. You cannot find comfort or meaning in something that never was. You must focus on what "is," and not on what "if." My wife chooses to focus on reality—and she has those real images and experiences "with her." In this way, she has her brother's life message and personality, with her.

You must prepare and strengthen yourself to continue the legacy and work of your parents, teachers and friends. Inevitably, your parents and teachers will leave this world, and you will be bereft of their physical and emotional guidance. You will then be alone. This is not living with a sense of morbid foreboding; rather it is living with an acceptance of reality. This may cause you to question your ability to survive without them since your emotional pillars and main support system have departed. However, if you reflect on the teachings, guidance and legacy of your parents, mentors and friends, and resolve to continue their values and legacy, then you will not be alone. Their legacy will continue through your actions—and they will be with you in everything you do. Spiritually, they will accompany you on your journey.

Jenna 45, was a stroke rehabilitation nurse. She was a caring and compassionate individual who cared deeply about the people she treated in the rehab hospital. Jenna was married to Evan who was the love of her life. They had been high school sweethearts. They had no children and were completely devoted to each other. Evan developed cancer and they spent their last year together, cherishing every minute they had left.

Evan died and Jenna descended into a deep depression. She stopped working and went on welfare. She felt that could not go on without Evan and that life had lost its meaning. There was no point in living, she said, if we are all going to die.

Jenna was experiencing depression, inner turmoil, confusion, and a sense of worthlessness; she lost her sense of "self." It was as if she was in "exile" from herself. Jenna's thoughts were scattered and inconsistent, which led to losing her way forward. She shut down and withdrew from life.

In group therapy we discussed the ego, the "self" and the meaning of "identity." We introduced the concept of the ego and that if you can look beyond your own pain and within your inner being and psyche, you will find your "self." If you gain a consciousness of "self" then you will not allow yourself to be defined by the pain that you are experiencing. You become "bigger" than the pain.

Your *ego* means your desires, wants or will. If what I want is to enforce my desires or will on others then I am driven by self-interest and selfishness. The use of my ego—and only my ego—gives rise to an attitude that only I deserve to "be," and that others are subservient to my will. This is the ultimate conceit and leads to controlling and abusive relationships.

The opposite of self-interest is humility, where you consider your life to be a gift. When your humility is in exile from yourself—then power and conceit take over. You say to yourself, I don't deserve to lose someone. It is not fair. If I lost the love of my life then I refuse to go on. My ego is hurt and angry. How dare God or the universe take my loved one away from me. I refuse to continue to participate in life. This ego-based anger leads to depression.

With this attitude and world-view you try to compensate for the anger by becoming self-absorbed and over-thinking. You withdraw into yourself and emotionally isolate yourself. You then feel disconnected from others and that is why you become irritable, angry and depressed. The depression is anger turned inward, against yourself. This further disconnects you from others and makes you feel like an outsider.

Ironically, to heal from the exile from yourself, you must become existentially alone, but not in a disconnected way. You must begin to see yourself as alone and unique. You become alone with an attitude of humility that despite the pain you do have a life mission and a purpose to fulfill. With this type of aloneness of humility, you become conscious of your innate value, and potential for goodness, and become motivated to make a unique contribution to others.

The aloneness of humility is a struggle for emotional independence; the opportunity to be free of a self-absorbed ego and self-interest. This struggle for independence, then, is the epic human struggle for selfhood. It is the "self," struggling with "itself," to decide which values and ethics to live by. Instead of being a negative matter, therefore, the inner struggle with your ego is symbolic of the basic struggle of the human condition, which cannot be avoided. Rather, it is a necessary battle—a search for identity. It is as a result of this essential inner struggle, that you can identify the ego and, at least in the moment of that awareness, tame the ego, and channel your inner self—your consciousness, to choose good and to make healthy choices.

The selfish ego urges you to be independent of morality and ethics—and to become your "own" man. Your ego tells you that you are a "self-made" man. Your conscious self, or power of Free Will, however, seeks independence from that very ego, and strives to serve a purpose beyond yourself—beyond your own self-interest.

How do you discover your own conscious self? When you relinquish what you "have." When you leave the concept of "having," you will arrive at the reality of "being." This is much more than having or owning things. It is experiencing reality itself. When you remove the distractions of materialism, jealousy, and honor from within your ego, you reveal your true independent self. You now arrive at an existential aloneness—and access your Free Will. The ego holds you back from discovering your inner self. By identifying the self-interest motives of your own ego, you arrive at a state of consciousness, which frees you up to seek a sense of purpose and destiny. In order to reach the core reality of self, you have to go deeper into your psyche than cravings for sensual pleasures; you have to discover your core beliefs and discover what you are living for.

One of the raw goals of the ego is to seek to master, mold and shape the material world for personal financial and physical benefit. When you become "conscious," you learn to let go of mastering the world of materialism—and focus on the reality of who you really "are." When you let go of what you have or own, you are forced to come face-to-face with your own "being."

With our preoccupation with entertainment and

recreational activities we are subconsciously avoiding and distracting ourselves from having to face our true inner selves. That is why psychologists are now suggesting that families unplug from technological devices and spend twenty-four hours bonding with each other and getting in touch with their inner thoughts and emotions.

This process of self-discovery can be a daunting, anxiety-producing endeavor. We are often afraid to confront our inner fears and unresolved emotions, for then we would have to deal with that which we might find. Consciousness, however, is the process whereby your "self" becomes the vehicle of self-actualization and fulfillment.

When you are conscious, even though challenging events can be swirling around you, your mind-set will be in the "zone," such that you will not allow external, challenging events, to define you. You will not allow your mood to be controlled by the particular challenge that you are currently facing. Your thoughts, which interpret an event, will often lead to an emotion such as fear, sadness or anger. But if you access your core self—your Free Will—then you will be able to choose to respond to these challenges—and deal with them from your own sense of self and identity. This is called consciousness.

Your inner turmoil is evidence of the ultimate battle for identity and self-definition. You are alone in this battle—and it is only in that aloneness, that you will find your "self." You will then discover the breadth of personality and "selfhood" to integrate aloneness within your "self," such that your "I" is bigger than the pain of your loneliness. You can take your identity, self and Free Will, and integrate your loneliness within your "self," and thereby not allow life's challenges to define you. Rather, your conscious self can endure, grow from, and learn from life's challenges. Then you will be conscious enough to define your own "self," and not be defined by the emotional challenge that you are currently facing.

EIGHTEEN

Self-Reflection

Zane is 38, and has been a drug dealer, drug addict, pimp and hit man. He has done significant jail time. He came to our clinic to treat his depression. During Conscious Therapy we did an empty chair experiential exercise where Zane symbolically placed his drug addict "self" in the empty chair in front of him, and had a "conversation" with himself, going back and forth between the two chairs. Chair A was his good "self," the part of him that wants to change and be a good partner to his girlfriend and daughter. Chair B was the part of him that wants to return to the streets and get back to being a kingpin drug dealer and run the town. This is how the conversation went:

Drug Lord Self: You and I both know that this attempt to go straight won't last. We both know who you really are. You are full of it. You are a killer. You have ruined lives, including your own. You have seen too many brothers get blown up to clear your mind. You are done, man.

Clean Self: You're right. I am done…with that life. I have a five year old daughter and I don't want my daughter to grow up and marry someone like you.

Drug Lord Self: Too late, man. You are stuck in who you are and what you have done. Your reputation follows you. You know your name on the street. You are "The Facer." Your daughter will know soon enough who you really are.

Clean Self: I am going to teach her that people can change and that she can choose a good life. I am choosing a clean life, now. I am not going back to being you.

When the members of the therapy group witnessed this conversation, many of the other group members cried. Introspection is an exercise in self-analysis. Zane was willing to delve within himself, to the depths of his own internal pain and discovered that he had no-one to blame for his despair—but himself. His own ego created a disconnect from his own Free Will—and only Zane himself could repair that distance by taking responsibility for his choices.

This type of introspection—a searing personal self-reflection, must be done alone. This is not communal confession, or a feel-good sensitivity session. This is Zane confronting his inner turmoil—his inner-self, and coming to terms with who he is—and to live with himself. This is man's duty in "his" world—to discover himself and why he is here in the world, at this point in time.

Since each person has unique strengths and abilities, each of us has a mission to bring out a particular dimension of goodness in the world. Therefore, a person's "name," is "his destiny. On the streets Zane was known as "The Facer." It gave him a handle on selfhood, albeit a notorious one. But, Zane's "Facer" identity was now being challenged—by his newly emerging conscious self.

Zane discovered, through a searing moral inventory that he had a unique positive contribution to make to the world. Your contribution may be a business, a unique way to be of service to others, the development of a particular unique character trait, a way to teach character development, an act of kindness, or the founding of a new charitable organization. It is something that only you—alone—are meant to bring to the world. Your contribution can be actualized by your introspecting and discovering the unique contribution that your inner self reveals to you. Introspection involves asking yourself, *What dormant strength is there within me that I am meant to discover and reveal?* Thus, your inner struggle, pain and challenge will lead you to discover your destiny.

Zane was battling to develop a sense of independence, internal drive, and vision, to enable him to resist the influences around him and to achieve his unique destiny. Zane strove to forge an independent identity—alone and unique in his ideas, values and character traits, distinct from the destructive influences of the street. And Zane discovered that his life mission and destiny was to overcome his addiction and peer pressure, and to show himself, his family and the community that change is possible, especially when it is improbable.

When you are alone against the world and your back is against the wall, you come face to face with yourself, and

your true self emerges. Your true self is your inner will—
what you truly desire. Introspection and mindfulness in a
time of despair, reveals that inner will. Your true self arises
out of and as a response to, your aloneness. Zane did not
experience the *aloneness* of facing himself in order to wallow
in guilt and self-deprecation. Instead, he used his newly
discovered consciousness to stand "alone," and to protect
someone else—his daughter.

Of course, there are unfortunate times when one
experiences the emotional pain of loneliness. A person who
is widowed, a widower, an orphan, a person who is single,
or a couple who have not been blessed with children—are
legitimately and understandably prone to feeling sad, hurt
and rejected. People need people—and these individuals are
suffering form excruciating emotional loneliness.

The silence of an empty house without children and
without a loved one is deafening and emotionally devastating,
beyond words. The emotional isolation and alienation
creates a silence of despair. The pain can be unbearable. In
the midst of our isolation and heartache we feel emotional
emptiness—how can we go on?

We must find, in the midst of our disconnection, the
meaning and growth that emerges from Conscious Solitude.
This is conscious state of being that is directed toward a sense
of purpose and destiny. Without this sense of conscious
purposefulness, Zane realized that his life was becoming
meaningless pleasure seeking. With consciousness, Zane
took a step toward transforming his life into a search for
meaning and contribution.

Whenever someone experiences something unusual, or

outside the norm, it is evident that this is a wake-up call. When we are singled out and faced with the challenge of *aloneness*, it can take on meaning despite the emotional loneliness. At such times, it is our mission and challenge to discover the personal character growth that we can extract and learn from such an experience.

When presenting us with the challenge of *aloneness*, the universe "wants something from us"—individually, uniquely. That is why each of us, alone, is often singled-out and placed in a position of emotional pain and loneliness. This is because the universe is urging us to bring out something from within us that would otherwise remain dormant, in order to make our unique contribution to the world.

NINETEEN

A Directed Life

Sue Ellen, 65, had been a remedial reading specialist working with children with dyslexia and auditory processing problems. Over the years, she founded and developed remedial resource rooms in various schools, when these resources were relatively new in the field of special education. She had been an innovator and now she was forced to retire due to mandatory retirement rules of the school board. She lost her sense of structure and had nothing to do. There are only so many novels you can read and so many trips you can take to the grocery store. Sue Ellen became anxious, confused and depressed.

The goals of a directed life allow you to become focused on purpose and meaning, which is the antidote to loneliness. In terms of motivations for living, psychologist, Abraham Maslow, posited a Hierarchy of Needs to understand man's needs and motivation or growth. This theory, developed in

1945, remains valid today for understanding human motivation, management training, and personal development. This system helps us understand how and why man desires to fulfill his unique potential. The Hierarchy of Needs is depicted as increasing levels of motivation, on a pyramid:[4]

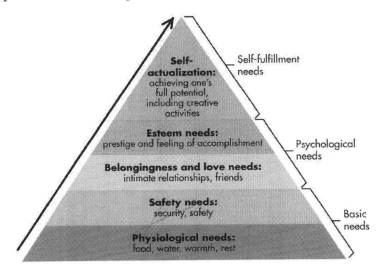

When faced with retirement Sue Ellen was confronted with an existential question: *Who am I? Other people are confronted by the same question when they face an existential challenge: If I have lost my spouse, who am I? If I have lost the security of my stock market savings, and my ego has been flattened, who am I? If I am left with only my "self," who am I?* Loneliness is resolved by achieving a consciousness of my own *aloneness*—and uniqueness. When I develop a consciousness of my own inner value and become productive, through volunteering to help others, taking on a hobby, writing a blog, or working for a charitable organization, I

4   www.simplypsychology.org/maslow.html, Saul McLeod, 2007, updated 2016

have something to live for.

When she was working, Sue Ellen introduced herself as a special education teacher. Once she retired and no longer had her career to identify her sense of purpose, she lost her sense of usefulness. She said, *I have lost myself.*

In the work of Conscious Therapy we explored the question, *Who am I?* We came up with a working definition, namely, the "I" is the combination of my body and my consciousness of my thoughts, feelings, hopes and fears. My body-self, which is the "me," is directed by my conscious self, which is the "I," to create selfhood. This means that when a person integrates her thoughts, feelings, and actions, and aligns them with her Free Will, she becomes conscious. Now Sue Ellen was able to think about what new contribution she wanted to make to the welfare of others. Life does not end at retirement.

The way to integrate and align these three aspects of "me," namely, thoughts, feelings and actions, is through the vehicle of Free Will, the "I." It is through this vehicle that Sue Ellen learned to activate her "I," will, or essence, to direct her cognitions to guide and channel her feelings, and in turn, to actualize them into good deeds. Consciousness is what gave Sue Ellen the intellectual will to transform good intentions into performance and self-actualization.

TWENTY

Free Will

Lance is a 32 year old journalist and author, who was diagnosed with Early Onset Parkinson's Disease, which is a long-term degenerative disorder of the central nervous system that mainly affects the motor system. The symptoms generally manifest slowly over time. Early in the disease, the most obvious symptoms are hand tremors, rigidity, slowness of movement, and difficulty with walking.[1] Thinking and behavioral problems may also occur. Dementia becomes common in the advanced stages of the disease.[2] Depression and anxiety are also common, occurring in more than one third of people with Parkinsons.[2] Other symptoms include sensory, sleep, and emotional problems. Lance was divorced and had one child whom he visited regularly. After his diagnosis, he began to question whether fighting to manage the illness was worth it, after all, it was going to eventually incapacitate him and his life expectancy was seven to fourteen years. Lance asked the ultimate question: I am going to die, so why does anything matter, anymore?

Man is the only being who is the source of his own actions through the exercise of his Free Will. The rest of the universe, i.e. animals, and systems of nature, are an expression of causes and effects that operate on them. Animals and systems of nature are bound by the framework of causes and effects.

Man is unique in the world, and there is no other species like him, as he is independent in his wisdom and his thoughts, knowing good and bad, and choosing what he desires, and there is no one who can prevent him from choosing to do either good or bad.

Man can choose to actualize himself by choosing to act with deliberate, informed and educated choices. Man is not bound by the framework of causes and effects, rather he is an originator. He can innovate and recreate himself. In this, man is alone. He makes his Free Will decisions alone, and independently creates his destiny; no-one else can do that for him. He does this with the power of Free Will. Your Free Will is the essence of what makes you human.

Consciousness means an awareness of the self as an independent, autonomous reality. This means self-awareness and being conscious of your independent existence. Instead of saying simply, "I have something," you can now say, "I have existence." When you exercise your Free Will to refrain from doing something that your heart desires, but you know will hurt someone else, then you have achieved awareness. When you choose to exercise your Free Will to do good, you gain true existence—and consciousness.

This means that everyone has the potential to actualize his or her highest and most noble self. Instead of being a slave to your desires, lusts, honor, and passions, you can choose to remain true to your higher purpose—service of others. You become "other centered" instead of "self-centered."

Each person has an obligation to create his own world, and destiny. We must create ourselves, through selfhood and self-mastery. We do this by integrating the concept of Free Will, and making it an ongoing theme in our lives. This is our goal; it our responsibility to strive for this on an ongoing basis.

Lance has the Free Will to continue managing his illness, to contribute to his child's wellbeing and education, and to enlighten people with his writing, for as long as he can, or he can chose to give up and let himself deteriorate. This is the ultimate Free Will, which is beyond choosing to travel to one place or another, or choosing to marry one person or another or, choosing whether to hurt someone, or not. Lance's Free Will centers around whether he wants to choose to live as best as he can, or whether he wishes to stop living. I taught Lance that we are all going to die, and the issue is what will be the content of the "dash" on his tombstone. He asked me what dash? I answered, you were born in 1985 and let's say you will die in 2085. Your tombstone will read,

Lance

1985-2085

The real significance of your tombstone is what you decide to put in the dash between the 1985 and 2085. Everything you decide to do in your lifetime will be represented by that dash. Will you decide to "live" that dash? What will your dash look like?

Selfishness creates a distance between your "me" and your

"I." According to a great Jewish philosopher, Simcha Bunim of P'Shischa, (1765–1827), everyone should have two pockets, each containing a slip of paper. On one should be written: "I am but dust and ashes," and on the other: "The world was created for me." From time to time we must reach into one pocket, or the other. The secret of living comes from knowing when to reach into each pocket.

Are these two slips of paper contradictory? No. You can resolve the apparent contradiction by taking your Free Will and submitting yourself to the service of others, meaningful projects, and making a difference, while you are here. When you do that, then far from being dust and ashes, you become connected to Everything. It is like a tile in a mosaic floor. It is one small tile, but when it is placed in the mosaic, it becomes part of a masterpiece. The tile's presence is essential for the mosaic to be whole. It contributes to the overall masterpiece while maintaining its own unique individuality. It is simultaneously an individual and part of the whole.

TWENTY-ONE

Worthiness

Daniel's parents died in a car accident when he was 5. He was brought up by his uncle and aunt. Daniel got into the wrong crowd and started smoking marijuana at age 13. He then graduated to harder drugs and became involved with cocaine at age 15, upon which his uncle threw him out of the house. He lived with various friends until he graduated from high school, with honors. He then became a roadie for a rock group and became a heroin addict. He contracted Hepatitis C and is now living with his girlfriend in a makeshift trailer which has no running water and a hole in the roof. He is on welfare. Our clinic recognized his sharp intellect and is encouraging him to find new accommodations and to get him help to finance a certificate course in computer programming. He feels emotionally alone and abandoned by his family and feels that the system has rejected him.

Daniel is experiencing the pain of existential loneliness. He feels detached from the world—that no one cares about him, and that his therapist only cares because he is getting paid by the State insurance plan. He experiences a condition called "dissociation"—the feeling that he is not really alive, not really here. People who have suffered severe trauma sometimes develop such a condition, in which they disconnect from themselves and feel that they are not really alive. Conscious Therapy provided Daniel with a reality check to bring him back into the world of the here and now, to verify that he is indeed alive and has survived the trauma.

The reason Daniel dissociates is to allow himself to come to terms with the trauma, otherwise he feels that he could not survive emotionally. The rejection by his uncle, brought his innate value, worth and very existence into doubt. In order to cope with the emotional pain, he enters a mental state where he feels he does not exist. In disconnecting from himself, he imagines that he is not here and his mind goes elsewhere. This is a defense mechanism to avoid the pain and trauma he experienced. In this way he does not have to face the reality of the emotional pain that he experienced. He disconnects from himself, and in turn from the pain. He has trained himself to become numb and to feel no emotions.

Many of us have experienced Daniel's sense of being scattered and disconnected from ourselves, at one time or another. Our thoughts and behavior are inconsistent; in one situation we act one way, and the next moment we "become" a different person. One minute we want one thing, but quickly lose focus and move on to something else. Disjointed, we embark upon one endeavor, but keep getting distracted, and end up jumping from one thing to the next. This is ADD—Attention Deficit Disorder. Consciousness is a charge for me to gather all of my disparate components, thoughts and emotions and to begin to walk a coherent, resolute and determined pathway, toward a goal and destiny.

We all cope with the emotional challenges of life with some minor form of dissociation. It is called depression. It is similar to dissociation in that we feel numb and disconnected from our emotions. The way to overcome this feeling of existential emptiness is to realize that you are not alone; you are inherently connected to your own consciousness. You can access your conscious self by identifying your strongest attribute, and use it in your relationships (Step Two of Conscious Therapy.) The awareness of that character trait and your striving to actualize it will ground you and center you emotionally, and allow you to become conscious of the fact that you have the innate ability to handle the challenge. In this way, in the midst of a challenge, you will not feel alone or abandoned, rather you can strive for consciousness by connecting with your best attribute and use it to cope with the challenge.

Getting in touch with your inner fears, pain, hopes and aspirations, means you have engaged with your inner "self." Your "me" self connects with your core "I" self (William James, 1897). This is the meaning of hearing your "self" or hearing your inner music; it is called consciousness.

When you resolve to live consciously—through positive speech and good deeds, you are effectively saying that you have a unique mission and contribution to make in building the reality around you, and are thus contributing your words and deeds—to make the world a better place.

If you see yourself as "self-made," you would never grow; you would not be motivated to grow in character or improve. You would stagnate in your own arrogance. When you are "self-made," you can misperceive reality. You may come to live in your own "reality." In other words, you will consider only yourself and will not go beyond your own "self."

When you find a sense of purpose, you uplift yourself above simply "exisiting," and you raise yourself up to a transcendent reality. At these times your sense of "self" expands; you become a "bigger" person; a greater version of yourself. You then gain an expanded sense of consciousness. The feeling you get when you grow from one level of "self," and character, to the next—an expanded version of self—is fulfillment. Thus, growth leads to true happiness—an inner joy that arises within, from the knowledge that you have become a bigger person whose character has developed and improved.

You can expand your consciousness and become a "bigger" person by growing in character as a result of the challenge you are facing. The feeling that arises within you when you grow in character is inner contentment and joy. If you refrain from saying the negative comment that you might otherwise say, or refrain from raising your voice, showing anger or speaking ill of someone, you expand your consciousness. The feeling of accomplishment that arises within your psyche when you go outside your comfort zone, is one of expansiveness and growth; and you thus come closer to achieving your purpose and destiny. That gives rise to inner joy. Here are some of the innate character traits that you have, and which you can develop:

Consistency: Is your love of your spouse, children and parents consistent? Do you persevere in your love even if you are hurt? Do you follow through in giving unconditional love, even if you do not get love in return?

Strong Will: Do you live by the strength of your convictions? Do you stand up for what you believe? Do you take a stand for what is right? Do you live by your values or do you merely pay them lip service?

Compassion. Do you feel and show compassion for family members, friends, neighbors and community? Do you feel the plight of the less fortunate?

Empathy: Are you gracious and loving? Or do your smiles mask your true feelings? You can tell whether someone has empathy: just look at their eyes. Are their eyes smiling or just their lips? Do you feel true empathy for the emotional pain of others?

Patience: Are you patient with your spouse, parents and children? Most people are pretty intense. However, if you work on your patience, you will grow in humility.

Kindness: There are some people who cannot do enough, who are constantly doing for others and looking for ways to be of service.

Truth: How careful are you about gossiping? Do you work on expressing positive words of praise and encouragement of others? Do you go out of your way to be positive with your speech? This takes effort—to look for the good and be proactive in praising and encouraging others.

Creativity: Do you think creatively? Do you have creative or innovative ideas for your family, friends and community? Do you create projects and charitable campaigns?

Forgiving: Do you forgive those who have hurt you? Do you let go of resentments? How long do you feel you need to hold on to that feeling of being insulted and hurt? Ask yourself, what is the payoff or benefit in holding on to the anger and resentment? Are you looking for justice? Do you want to play the victim? Are you looking for an apology, or sympathy?

Resilience: It is your job to take a personal inventory of your strengths in order to discover your life mission and stay on track despite setbacks. Can you bounce back from setbacks and difficulties? Can you learn from the setback and move on with a renewed sense of purpose and meaning?

TWENTY-TWO

Fear of Death

Gabriella, 33, is married with two children. She is a talented teacher who works in the inner city school system and her goal is to make a difference and improve the lives of challenged children. She has a good marriage and is very close with her parents. She lives 300 miles from her parents and misses them. She sometimes regrets having moved away and is concerned that her parents are getting older. Five years ago, her grandmother, with whom she was very close, passed away, suddenly. She has become anxious about death and fears losing her own parents. She fears "getting that phone call," and being "blindsided by death." This anxiety and obsessional fear of death is getting in the way of her healthy functioning. She came to my private practice for counseling.

In working through the steps of Conscious Therapy with Gabriella, we elaborated on Step 7, Choosing Love over

Fear, in order to address Gabriella's obsessional thinking about death. The fear of losing her parents incapacitated Gabriella and sapped her enjoyment of life. She was unable to "live in the moment" and enjoy spending time with her parents and children because she obsessed over the thought that "this might be the last time I ever see them."

The obessional thinking was robbing Gabriella of her enjoyment of life. The thoughts, which we diagnosed as OCD—Obsessional Compulsive Disorder, were overwhelming her to the extent that she could not focus on her daily tasks, her teaching, or her kids. The OCD was not a physical/compulsive condition where people wash their hands many times per day, or check the door many times to make sure it is locked. This was a thinking obsession. In other words, the compulsion was her obsessional thinking. Her obsessional thinking robbed her of being conscious of the moment.

In order to manage and overcome obsessional thinking the optimum therapy is called Exposure and Response Prevention Therapy. In this technique Gabriella and the therapist together create a written script which Gabriella will read five times a day in order to expose herself to the fear of death, and then do absolutely nothing about her fears; rather she will simply "sit with" the feeling of fear and learn to cope with it, without reacting to it. The technique is called Exposure and Response Prevention Therapy because Gabriella must learn to expose herself to the fear and not perform any avoidance, distraction, or reassurance actions, to calm her anxiety. She must cope with the inevitable fears connected with living, and not run from them, otherwise the fear will control her and she will become overwhelmed by the fear. The second dimension of the therapy is called Response Prevention because Gabriella must learn to tolerate her fear and get used to it without rationalizing or running from it. Here is the script that Gabriella and I crafted:

My greatest fear is that I am going to die. And if I die the people that depend on me will be left helpless. So when I plan to work out or go to the gym I never really follow through or get there because I am worried about what will happen when I get there. So, in essence what is holding me back from happiness is the fear of the unknown, and uncertainty of the future. I cannot control the outcome so I am afraid to move forward.

If I think about it, there are many uncertainties in my life. My baby's health, my health, my parent's health, my job security, and my marriage, are all uncertain; I don't know what is going to happen with any of these situations. There are no guarantees. There may be a hurricane, a tornado or a another 9/11 terrorist attack, or civil war about America's political divide. Maybe there will be one of these scenarios and maybe there won't. I can't be sure.

I have learned to tolerate and live with the uncertainty of these possibilities because I realize that certainty is an illusion. There is no such thing as a certainty or a guarantee of safety or security. I have learned to tolerate these uncertainties in my life and I will learn to tolerate my fear and uncertainty of dying.

I am willing to face the uncertainty of going to the gym and maybe being attacked. If that happens, I will:
  Get help;
  Be mortally wounded;
  Survive;
  Fight back;
  Take a self-defense course.

If any of these things happen I will face this reality and move past it. I am willing to face the possibility and learn to live with the uncertainty and tolerate the possibility that one of these things might happen. Since it is possible that I will die, I will make provisions in my will for my child to be taken care of by my husband. If we both die, we will make provisions for my parents to take care of our child. I will learn to face the somber possibilities and cope with them. I will deal with and face reality without distracting myself or avoiding the possibilities. I will tolerate uncertainty because uncertainty is part of the fabric of living.

Gabriella read the script five times a day and initially it caused an increase in her anxiety. It is supposed to make her more anxious at first, since she is exposing herself to her fear of death, and that scares her. But once she flooded herself with the notion that death is a reality, and that it is part of life, she realized that the only thing she can do is: "deal with it." There is nothing she can do about the reality of death, other than to accept that reality. She can take whatever steps she can to stay healthy, work out, eat healthy and carry on a healthy lifestyle; in other words, to put in her best efforts to live as long she can, in a healthy manner. But more than that, she cannot do. She must accept that, and live with the reality that one day her parents will die, and one day she will die.

Gabriella's fear of death so preoccupied her mind that it interfered with her healthy functioning and day to day living. Once she used the Exposure and Response Prevention technique, she was able to manage her thoughts and deal with them. We utilized the technique as part of Step 7 of Conscious Therapy to allow her to choose Love of Reality over the Fear of Death. The work she did by reading the script five times a day for two weeks, allowed her to become "conscious" again by putting her fears in perspective and allowing her to resume healthy daily functioning while being aware of the reality of death. In this sense, she regained "consciousness" and was able to resume normal functioning.

TWENTY-THREE

Challenges Create Consciousness

Ryan, 44, is a marketing consultant with a major investment bank. He is married with two children, ages 9 and 5. His parents were divorced when he was 12. His parents were distant and not demonstrative or expressive of their love for him or his siblings. They were hands-off, aloof and stand-off-ish in their parenting style but did provide shelter and an education for their kids. Ryan needed attention and sought it from the wrong crowd of teen friends. This peer group got good at "taking" their respective parent's liquor stash, partying and binge drinking. At 19 Ryan became an alcoholic and dropped out of college at age 20. He joined AA at age 27 and got sober at age 30. He was clean for 3 years when he married Helen who was also a recovering alcoholic. Since Helen was not a "morning person," Ryan would do the morning shift, clean up the dinner dishes from the night before, feed the kids breakfast, read to the kids and get them off to school, before he went to work. After a few years of this and having spoken with his friends, he began to resent this morning routine and wondered why he was stuck being "Mr. Mom," while his friends were at the gym at 7 AM. He began to make demands of Helen and their marriage began spiraling out of control. Ryan came to see me in my private practice for counseling.

During Conscious Therapy I introduced Ryan to the concept that consciousness required a sense of individuality and independent thinking in order for him to resist the urge to conform to the "norms" of others. Ryan agreed that his marriage situation was unique and that he would have to stop comparing his relationship to that of his friends. Ryan concluded that if his wife needed his help in the mornings, then that took him out of the category of a "7 AM workout guy." It is not a question of Ryan looking over his shoulder jealously at his friend's workout schedule. Rather, gaining consciousness required Ryan to appreciate and understand his own uniqueness, and to accept that helping his wife in the mornings was his "destiny" and that it was in his own best interest. Helping his wife was the best thing for his relationship, and had nothing to do with being a wimp or "being controlled" by his wife, as his friends suggested. Sometimes the peer pressure exerted by friends can interfere with your relationship.

Then, Ryan and I took Conscious Therapy to a deeper level. I asked Ryan to reflect on why his marriage challenge was actually "good" for him. His initial reaction was that marriage conflict is not good for anyone. I challenged him by saying that a challenge may not be fun or pleasant but it could still be "good" if it helped him grow. If the purpose of life is happiness then marriage conflict cannot be good because it makes us unhappy, which contradicts our stated purpose in life. But, if the purpose of life is not happiness, but "meaning" through growth in character, then life challenges actually push us to grow—and that is a good thing.

I asked Ryan to think about the correlation between his life's unresolved "unfinished business," and the particular marriage conflict that he was experiencing. Ryan said that his unfinished business was his low self-esteem stemming from the fact that his father—the key person from whom he had sought approval—was not particularly loving and demonstrative toward him. Furthermore, every morning, due to his mother's anxiety, she would yell at him, criticize, and was obsessively "on his case" due to his inability to get going smoothly in the mornings. Ryan would go to school every morning feeling horrible and in tears. As a result, Ryan felt empty, unloved and rejected.

In his teens and twenties Ryan sought to numb the pain of feeling unworthy and unloved by turning to alcohol. During Conscious Therapy, Ryan came to realize that the conflict with his wife was part of the process of resolving the unfinished business and pain of his childhood. By accepting, optimizing and leveraging the fact that his wife was not a morning person, Ryan could now become a key player in his children's lives by being loving and demonstrative to them in the mornings during their formative years by sending them off to school feeling good about themselves. In this way, Ryan was given the opportunity to give his children that which he never got, namely, unconditional love and attention. Ryan realized that he was able to heal his own "unfinished business" of the pain of his childhood, by giving attentive, sensitive love to his own children. Recently, Ryan has been making breakfast for Helen, and leaving it for her in the kitchen with a loving note. In this way Ryan's marital challenge became the trigger, catalyst and creator of Ryan's growth and consciousness. That which Ryan resented, actually became an opportunity for him to grow. Because of Ryan's conscious growth, his children do not have to suffer that which he did. Ryan moved from being merely awake, to being conscious.

Tyree is 33, and grew up in the "hood" without a father. He did not realize the impact that life without a father had on him, until he met his father for the first time when he was 14. He and his mother were walking together and saw his father across the street, and Tyree's mother said, "Oh, there's your father." At that moment, an unexplained feeling of rage surged through Tyree, and he ran across the street, punched his father in the back of the head, and started crying in frenzied agitation. As he grew up, Tyree attributed all of his setbacks, including failing out of school, having a daughter at age 19, not being allowed to visit or interact with his daughter, failed relationships and failing out of technical school, to his pain and anger at his father for having abandoned him and his siblings. Tyree broke his hand three times, having slammed his fist into brick walls, and a few family friends suggested that he should learn to control his angry outbursts. Tyree came to our clinic for counseling.

After a few preliminary sessions, I asked Tyree what he was so angry about. He said he was angry at the world for having made him fail at life. I asked him if his "angry at the world" approach to life was working for him, and he said that it helped him calm down. I then asked him if he was planning to move forward with his life, and he said he was stuck in his past. I asked him to place his anger in the "empty chair" in front of him and "talk" to the anger, and he began to cry. He told his angry self that it is all his father's fault and that whenever he would next see his father he would hurt him.

The empty chair exercise went on for a while and Tyree told his angry self that he never realized that his anger had such power over his life, and that he didn't know any other way of getting the anger out. I intervened in the chair dialogue and suggested that Tyree tell his angry self that it could work with him instead of against him, by channeling his passion into winning at life—and that would be his revenge over his father. Tyree negotiated with his anger, got to know the source of his anger, and decided to take back control of his life.

Through the use of the Wheel of Strengths, of Step One of Conscious Therapy (page 26), we helped Tyree work on recognizing and developing his positive character traits and life goals. Tyree soon decided that after he went back to school and became a successful businessman, he wanted to reestablish the teen community centers which had closed in his neighborhood. He said he wanted to hire youth workers who could serve as "father figures" for the youth, many of whose fathers were absentee fathers, who had abandoned their families. Tyree said that if the teens had role models and something constructive to do with their time they would be less likely to turn to drugs and crime.

I asked Tyree what the correlation was between the unfinished business of the pain of his teen years, and his life goal of providing role models for inner-city teens. He said that he didn't want his life-story to be repeated by others. He then had an insight: perhaps his life goal of helping teens would be the antidote which would help heal his own pain. Instead of seeing himself as "rejected," he could reframe it and consider himself "redirected" to emerge from the pain and transform himself into someone who healed the pain, of others. Not rejected, but redirected. I told Tyree that perhaps his life challenge had become his destiny and that it could be the catalyst to make a difference in the lives of many youth. Tyree's emotional pain triggered his journey toward consciousness.

TWENTY-FOUR

Finding Your Voice

Emily is a 41 year old professor of English in a Southern university. Her parents died in a car accident when she was 6 and she was raised by her grandparents. When she was 8 she was sexually abused by a "doting" uncle which abuse lasted until she was 15. When she was 17 she had her first boyfriend, whom she liked because "he liked me and paid attention to me. I needed love and validation. I didn't really have any other substantial reason to like him." When she was 18 she got pregnant by her boyfriend and when she was 8 months pregnant he left her for a 27 year old divorcee. He did not attend the birth of Emily's child. She was devastated by the betrayal. She went to university and got her Bachelor's Degree in English, and at 22 had a second baby by a new boyfriend, who left her when the baby was 3 months old. At 25 she married a man who failed to work and support the family and whom she divorced four years later.

At 27 she got her Masters in English Literature and enrolled in a PhD program. At 35 she got her PhD and began teaching at a university. She entered into a relationship with a fellow professor who had various liaisons through social media with other women. She ended the relationship and came to therapy asking why she was stuck in pattern of relationships with men who kept abandoning her.

When we began Conscious Therapy, Emily promised herself that she would not allow herself to be hurt again and decided she would never enter into another relationship. She was "done." During Inner Child work (Step Six of Conscious Therapy, page 47,) we delved into the pain of abuse that Emily experienced in her childhood, and spent many sessions processing that she felt worthless, and that she saw herself as merely an instrument of pleasure for men. She had no sense of "self," no voice, and felt her opinions or needs did not count. During therapy we focused on Emily's intellectual and character traits (The Wheel of Strengths, Step One of Conscious Therapy, page 28,) and how she was entitled to choose whom to love. She slowly began to gain a voice and learned that although her body had been abused, her essence, or conscious self was intact.

We reviewed Emily's pattern of men professing love for her and then abusing or abandoning her. Emily discovered that the loss of her parents and the resulting loss of attention and guidance, left her feeling alone and unworthy of love. Her grandparents were unable to relate to her, "get her," or guide her. She portrayed herself as needy and desperate for love and men took advantage of her vulnerability.

I asked Emily to draw a flow chart of the challenges and successes in her life and it looked like this:

Death of parents
Abused by uncle
Left by first boyfriend
Give birth alone
Bachelor's degree
Second child
Betrayed by boyfriend
• *Masters degree*
Ph.D.
Betrayed by her Professor boyfriend
Raising responsible children

As she charted her challenges and successes, I asked her what the theme of her challenges was, and what she thought she was meant to learn from them? She said the theme was that she was needy and had no voice, and chose relationships only because men showed interest in her, and not because they possessed any values that she respected. I asked her whether she was ready to have a voice and choose what she wanted and deserved in a relationship. She said she developed a voice in her academic career and now she wanted a voice in her social life. For the first time, Emily was brave enough to articulate that she wanted a relationship with a man who had a work ethic, who was loyal and kind, and who knew how to be a role model to her boys.

By analyzing her pattern of challenges and reflecting on them, Emily was able to see that the challenges were "speaking" to her. Through Conscious Therapy, Emily recognized that the pattern of abuse and betrayal that she suffered was not a life-sentence; rather it was a life-challenge to respond to and to grow from. She decided she wanted to take on the identity of victor, instead of victim.

One of the key goals of Conscious Therapy is to use the theme and pattern of your life challenges as a catalyst and guide to discover your life mission. Once you chart and discover the pattern of your life-challenges, you can let them point you in the direction of which character strengths and attributes you already have within your psyche, which you can use to meet the challenge. With each challenge, your life attributes and personal resources are being strengthened and refined. Your life challenges can then be used as a "wake-up call" to become aware and conscious of your destiny; and when your dormant attributes begin to awaken, you can begin to live consciously.

TWENTY-FIVE

Self Disclosure

I took a short trip to Israel to visit our married children and grandchildren, and the return flight was scheduled to land in Newark, New Jersey at 4:15 AM on a Tuesday. I planned to take the Amtrak train which left at 8:30 AM from the Newark airport, and was scheduled to arrive in Baltimore at 10:43 AM.

I arranged with my wife that she would pick me up at the train station at 10:43 AM and planned to get home at 11 AM, take a shower and leave at 11:30 AM for work to arrive at work for my 12 noon clinic. That was the plan. My wife called me at 10:45 AM, after I arrived at the train station in Baltimore, and told me that she was a half a mile away from the train station but was on a one way street going away from the train station and could not find the entrance to the train station. I tried to guide her by MapQuest but she ended up getting lost and only got to the train station at 11:18 AM. That put me at home at 11:35 AM and I was not be able to get to work until 12:20 PM, unfortunately late.

When I got in the car at 11:18 AM, my wife asked me how my

trip was. I was working very hard on myself not to "lose it." I had hoped and planned to be at work that day at 12 noon. It would have been perfect had my wife not gotten lost. In fact, it should have been prefect had my wife used Waze or had done a dry run on Sunday to make sure she knew how to get there on time. After all, I am working to provide for our family and the least she could do is be there in time. Right? I was angry, but I did not raise my voice or show my anger. All I said when I got in the car was, "I need a few minutes to collect myself." I didn't say anything the whole ride home, while thinking to myself that if my wife really loved me she would have been there on time.

When I got to my clinic at 12:20 PM and began the group therapy session, late, the group happened to be discussing the topic of anger and self-control. In a moment of apparent weakness I de-cided to self-disclose to the group the story of my own anger of that morning, and my battle with myself not to "lose it" with my wife. During the group therapy session we worked out the following dia-gram, which dissects the process as to how and why I got angry, and how I could have done a better job in dealing with the situation.

Let us analyze each part of this diagram:

EXPECTATIONS
REALITY

My expectation was that my wife would arrive at 10:43 AM to pick me up. Reality was that she arrived at 11:18 AM. The distance or gap between my expectations and reality was 35 minutes of lateness. That distance caused me anxiety, frustration and anger. Why?

SHOULD HAVE
COULD HAVE
WOULD HAVE

I was angry and frustrated because had my wife been more efficient and organized she would have left earlier to pick me up, or she would have done a practice run on Sunday to make sure she knew the way, or used WAZE; then she would have been there on time and I would have gotten to work on time. My feeling was that she *could have* been there on time and that she *should have* been there on time. Why?

MY EGO

My ego says that she should have been there on time because in my opinion, my expectations were reasonable; we had discussed it, and she had agreed to pick me up because I wanted to save the $20 uber ride I would have had to pay had she not picked me up. After all, don't I "deserve" to be picked by a loving wife after having traveled 24 hours and not having slept but a few hours on a plane? After all, $20 is $20, isn't it? I mean, it doesn't really matter, in my opinion, that she had to change her schedule, try to figure out how to get to the train station even though she doesn't usually travel downtown, and even though she had to be at her teaching job at 12 noon and it put extra pressure on her, right? A husband has a right to get picked up by his wife, right?

MY LOW SELF ESTEEM

My ego was driven by the fact that if my wife really loved me she would have gone out of her way to pick me up on time. All this, "I Love you" talk is meaningless, unless a spouse can deliver the goods by doing a husband a favor, right? If she really loved me she would have been there, right? I don't really think she loves me, even though she says she does. If she really loved me she would have tried harder, don't you think?

ACCEPTANCE OF REALITY

In order to graduate from low self-esteem I need to accept the reality that life "happens," and that my wife is not perfect and she is entitled to be late, without me getting angry. Period. My low self-esteem caused to me to "interpret" her lateness as evidence that she did not love me. It is my low self-esteem which led me to make this distorted interpretation of "lack of love for me," since she came late. Had I had healthy self-esteem, I would have said, "Are you okay? I was worried about you. I hope you are not frustrated and anxious about being being late. It's okay. As long as you okay, that's what counts. Don't worry about it. I'll get there when I get there. Thanks for picking me up."

Unfortunately I didn't say that. I was self-absorbed and anxious about my being late and did not have the presence of mind to be concerned or to express concern about my wife's welfare. My ego was too preoccupied with my own self. In other words, my anxiety made me non-conscious. I was so fixated on my expectations and my fears of being late, that I did not want to accept reality.

That night at dinner, I apologized to my wife for not being concerned about her when I got in the car. I showed her the diagram that we had worked out in group therapy, and she said she was glad I calmed down and regained consciousness. I think I should re-read this book.

TWENTY-SIX

Believe in Yourself

When, therefore, a fellow creature needs your help and your blessing, bestow it freely without asking first whether he has deserved it? Shall you take umbrage at every offence and fume against it, instead of learning forbearance? Will you set so high a price on your love that not one in thousands should be worthy of it, so that the source of your love should run dry and your heart freeze and shrivel up? - Rabbi Samson Raphael Hirsh

Our task is to believe—and to know—that within the challenge and pain of anxiety, depression and loneliness, (ADL), there, you will find your true self. In fact, it is because of emotional pain, and your willingness and courage to face your existential *aloneness*, that you will be brave enough to explore your inner self and find your "self."

Once you enter, alone, into the emotional dark cloud

of emotional pain, you must keep going and come out the other side—as a transformed person. Your old needy self will have died, and you will emerge with a new perspective. You will discover that you no longer need parental approval or sympathy. You will now graduate into consciousness, destiny, purpose, and to making a contribution to others and to society.

The goal in life is to leave this world a better place than it was when you found it. You can drop the pain of loneliness, which is based on approval-seeking and needing love, and embrace the *aloneness* of giving and making a difference in the lives of others. You will graduate to living a life of contribution and you will exercise your Free Will to become a giver—and will you discover your "self." When you wake up and become fully conscious, you will have learned the art of being.

Research Data on the Effectiveness of Conscious Therapy
THE IMPACT OF CONSCIOUS THERAPY ON THE REDUCTION OF ANXIETY
YISROEL ROLL, MS, LCPC

Abstract

This study examines the impact of Conscious Therapy on clients suffering from Generalized Anxiety Disorder. A sample of 30 patients who are suffering from anxiety were selected to receive bi-weekly sessions of Conscious Therapy over a period of five months, for a total of ten sessions. For data collection The Hamilton Anxiety Rating Scale (HAM-A) and the Rosenberg Self-esteem Scale were used. The results indicated that those patients who performed the weekly homework of Conscious Therapy between therapy sessions reduced their self-reported anxiety symptoms by 3-73%. Those patients who did not perform the weekly Conscious Therapy homework did not reduce their anxiety symptoms.

1.0   Introduction: Conscious Therapy, developed by psychotherapist, Yisroel Roll, is a seven-step experiential therapy system which serves to develop a client's awareness and consciousness of the cognitive, emotional and behavioral dimensions of self. The seven step system is as follows:

Establishing the Conscious Self through awareness of the Cognitive, Emotional and Behavioral Dimensions of Self

1. Wheel of Strengths—Cognitive awareness by the client of her intellect, social skills, character traits, spirituality, family contribution and personal growth.

2. Soul State—an emotional awareness of a positive experience which places the client in a holistic, positive frame of experiencing the self.

3. Circle of Control—a behavioral awareness of what the client can do to respond to stimuli and events which are outside her locus of control.

Defending the Conscious Self from Cognitive and Emotional Attacks

4. Thought Highway—Client practices a mindfulness technique to recognize and allow negative thoughts to pass like trucks on a highway.

5. Becoming aware of Cognitive Distortions and replacing the distorted thinking with a positive mantra or affirmation.

6. Inner Child—Becoming aware of and healing

the emotional pain, and unfinished business of
childhood emotional pain so that the Inner Child
no longer controls the adult self.

Choosing to Operate with Free Will

7. Client chooses the approach of self love and
validation over the paralyzing fear of anxiety.

The interactive strategies and techniques presented
to the patient require him to perform daily homework journaling exercises.

2.0   Hypothesis: As a result of a course of 10 sessions of
        Conscious Therapy there would be a reduction in the
        client's symptoms of anxiety as the client's conscious-
        ness of self-value and self-esteem increased.

3.00   Methodology: The sample was a group of 30 clients
        at a mental health clinic in Baltimore, MD who had
        been diagnosed with Generalized Anxiety Disorder,
        Bipolar II, and/or Substance Abuse who were pre-
        scribed between 3 and 6 mgs per day of Xanax.

4.00   On intake each participant completed the Hamil-
        ton Anxiety Rating Scale (HAM-A) and the Rosen-
        berg Self–esteem Scale. The Hamilton Anxiety
        Rating Scale (HAM-A) is a widely used 14-item
        clinician-administered rating tool in the public do-
        main used to measure the severity of anxiety symp-
        toms among individuals previously diagnosed with
        anxiety disorders (McDowell, 2006). The HAM-A
        was originally developed by Max Hamilton in 1959

as an assessment tool to evaluate anxiety symptoms among people diagnosed with "anxiety neurosis." Since that time, anxiety neurosis has been re-conceptualized and the HAM-A is used among individuals with a variety of anxiety disorders (panic, phobia, and generalized) (McDowell, 2006). The 14 items reflect 13 categories of anxiety-related symptoms including anxious mood, tension, fear, insomnia, intellectual/cognitive symptoms, depressed mood, general somatic (muscular and memory symptoms), cardiovascular, respiratory, genitourinary, and gastrointestinal symptoms, with one item capturing the rater's assessment of behavioral symptoms. McDowell, I. (2006). *Measuring health: A guide to rating scales and questionnaires* (3rd ed.). New York: Oxford University Press.

The Rosenberg Self–Esteem Scale is a 10-item scale that measures global self-worth by measuring both positive and negative feelings about the self. The scale is believed to be uni-dimensional. All items are answered using a 4-point Likert scale format ranging from strongly agree to strongly disagree. Developed by Dr. Morris Rosenberg in 1959, The Rosenberg Self-Esteem Scale is a widely used self-reporting instrument for evaluating individual self-esteem. Gray-Little, B., Williams, V.S.L., & Hancock, T. D. (1997). An item response theory analysis of the Rosenberg Self-Esteem Scale. Personality and Social Psychology Bulletin, 23, 443-451.

5.00 Procedure: On intake into a voluntary anxiety therapy group, clients were asked to complete the Hamilton Anxiety Rating Scale (HAM-A) and the Rosenberg Self–esteem Scale and were told that the goal of the group was to learn techniques to reduce their anxiety symptoms. The clients were told that the optimum way to reduce anxiety is to do the anxiety therapy homework in the program they were about to embark upon called Conscious Therapy and were asked to be diligent in attending the ten week program and to do the homework assigned between sessions. The clients were told that their self-esteem and their anxiety would be assessed at the beginning of the study and again at after the tenth session. The results of a client's level of self-esteem culled from the Rosenberg Scale were tabulated and correlated to the results of the client's anxiety level culled from the Hamilton Anxiety Scale. The Anxiety Scale results are not raw scores, rather they were converted proportionately to a score out of 100, as follows:

6.00 Results

		Upon Intake		After 10 Weeks		% increase in self-esteem/ consciousness	% reduction in anxiety
		ROSENBERG	HAMILTON	ROSENBERG	HAMILTON		
1.	C	18	8	25	2	28%	75%
2.	A	13	20	16	8	18%	60%
3.	R	11	89	24	80	54%	11%
4.	D	17	42	25	30	32%	28%
5.	JD	10	50	12	21	16%	42%
6.	H	19	14	26	10	27%	20%
7.	D	14	19	19	10	26%	47%
8.	KM	8	66	12	40	17%	39%
9.	L	23	14	28	10	17%	28%
10.	D	16	37	24	32	33%	13%
11.	RD	7	71	6	87	- 18%	+ 14%
12.	MM	13	51	20	29	35%	43%
13.	L	6	80	11	64	45%	20%
14.	JM	19	57	26	35	26%	38%
15.	DL	21	60	23	21	8%	38%
16.	CR	16	57	24	12	33%	78%
17.	J	15	14	10	34	- 33%	+ 58%
18.	NK	7	38	6	63	- 14%	+ 65%
19.	K	14	24	24	17	41%	29%
20.	D	10	71	8	81	- 28%	+12%
21.	AM	5	69	11	64	54%	7%
22.	S	9	76	15	65	40%	14%
23.	CV	7	50	19	38	42%	24%
24.	S	9	53	9	62	0%	+ 14%
25.	T	17	50	14	58	- 17%	+ 16%
26.	D	9	51	8	55	- 11%	+ 7%
27.	MH	10	80	6	77	- 40%	3%
28.	CB	20	78	28	58	28%	25%
29.	TJ	22	62	27	47	18%	25%
30.	HL	18	87	27	17	33%	81%

7.00 Discussion:

This study investigates the correlation between consciousness and anxiety. It was hypothesized that increased consciousness, herein defined as self awareness, self-understanding, self-confidence and self-esteem, would reduce symptoms of anxiety. Research has shown that increased self-awareness leads to a reduction in the severity of anxiety.

The major findings elicited that adherence to a program designed to increase consciousness was a predictor of reduced anxiety and better interpersonal functioning. Consciousness of a client's cognitive, emotional and behavioral dimensions leads to "selfhood." When a client discovers a sense of "self," she can more readily cope with and handle a presenting challenge by marshalling her cognitive, emotional and behavioral strengths to solve or to cope with the challenge; this reduces the anxiety attendant upon the stressful process of dealing with a psychosocial stressor.

The strategy analyzed by this study is a new seven step experiential therapy approach called Conscious Therapy and its psychotherapy practitioners are called Conscious Therapists. This experiential/Gestalt therapeutic approach teaches a client about the formation of selfhood and the components of self, namely his mind, feelings and actions. The feelings are the central, driving force of personality and Conscious Therapy guides a client to make a "conscious choice" between reacting with an instinctive, impulsive body response, or, reacting with a mind-based, thoughtful, cognitive response. Conscious Therapy helps a client access the "self" or "I," in order to direct the "me," and to react to the crisis or challenge in a conscious, healthy manner, thus reducing anxiety that is usually associated with dealing with stressful situations.

Three categories of attacks to the client's new-found sense of sense are reviewed and presented to the client by the Conscious Therapist including Negative Thoughts, Cognitive Distortions and the unresolved pain of the client's Inner Child. The Conscious Therapist provides the client with techniques to respond to and manage these attacks to selfhood, which keep anxiety from overwhelming the client. Once the client learns and becomes adept at the system of defending against these attacks, the client can then choose a positive response to the challenge, rather than an anxiety based response.

In order to become adept at Conscious Therapy, the client is encouraged to complete nightly journaling homework assignments, which take 5-10 minutes per night. When the client does the homework, the client learns to utilize the Conscious Therapy techniques in real-time, and reports back to the Conscious Therapist her successes and failings in dealing with the challenges she encountered. The Conscious Therapist can then guide the client to modify or apply the seven Conscious Therapy techniques, in a more effective manner.

Over a period of ten sessions, occurring once every two weeks, our sample of thirty (30) clients, each of whom was suffering from Generalized Anxiety Disorder, Schizophrenia, or Bipolar II, twenty-three (23) of the clients performed the Conscious Therapy homework at least three times per week. Those clients raised their Consciousness Score, as monitored by the Rosenberg Self Esteem Scale, by 8% to 40%. Those same clients showed a reduction in anxiety, as monitored by the Hamilton Anxiety Scale, by 3% to 75%. Those clients who attended the ten Conscious Therapy sessions but did not perform the Conscious therapy homework, (namely Client Numbers 11, 17, 18, 20,24, 25 and 26, as per the results noted above) reduced their Consciousness Score, as monitored by the Rosenberg Self Esteem Scale, by 11% to 43%. Those same clients showed an increase in anxiety, as monitored by the Hamilton Anxiety Scale, by 7% to 58%.

The results of this study lead to the conclusion that individuals with Generalized Anxiety Disorder, Schizophrenia, or Bipolar II, who engage in homework-based Conscious Therapy for ten weeks will experience an increase in Consciousness and a reduction in anxiety.

Limitations of this study are that the Rosenberg Self Esteem Scale, and the Hamilton Anxiety Scale are self-reporting tools which were completed by the clients themselves, rather than by objective third-party observation or monitoring, i.e, doctor, nurse, spouse, friend, teacher. Furthermore, the sample did not monitor clients suffering from a sole diagnosis of Generalized Anxiety Disorder, rather the sample included those suffering from Generalized Anxiety Disorder, Schizophrenia, or Bipolar II, who in all cases did report that they were experiencing severe anxiety and were taking between 3 and 6 mg of Xanax per day. Despite these limitations, this study has practical benefits for those who seek to reduce their own, or their client's anxiety. Following a strategy to increase self-awareness and consciousness, appears to provide a client with the inner fortitude and practical tools to reduce the severity of anxiety.

Rosenberg Self-Esteem Scale RSES

Instructions: Below is a list of statements dealing with your general feelings about yourself. There are four possible answers for each of the 10 questions, from "strongly agree" to "strongly disagree." Tap the box to indicate how strongly you agree or disagree with each statement.

		Strongly Agree	Agree	Disagree	Strongly Disagree
1	On the whole, I am satisfied with myself	3	2	1	0
2	At times, I think I am no good at all	0	1	2	3
3	I feel that I have a number of good qualities	3	2	1	0
4	I am able to do things as well as most other people	3	2	1	0
5	I feel I do not have much to be proud of	0	1	2	3
6	I certainly feel useless at times	0	1	2	3
7	I feel that I'm a person of worth, at least on an equal plane with others	3	2	1	0
8	I wish I could have more respect for myself	0	1	2	3
9	All in all, I am inclined to feel that I am a failure	0	1	2	3
10	I take a positive attitude toward myself	3	2	1	1

Hamilton Anxiety Scale (HAM-A)

The Hamilton Anxiety Scale (HAM-A) is a rating scale developed to quantify the severity of anxiety symptomatology, often used in psychotropic drug evaluation. It consists of 14 items, each defined by a series of symptoms. Each item is rated on a 5-point scale, ranging from 0 (not present) to 4 (severe).

0 = Not present   to   4 = Severe

Score _____

1. ANXIOUS MOOD
   • Worries
   • Anticipates worst

2. TENSION
   • Startles
   • Cries easily
   • Restless
   • Trembling

3. FEARS
   • Fear of the dark
   • Fear of strangers
   • Fear of being alone
   • Fear of animal

4. INSOMNIA
   • Difficulty falling asleep
     or staying asleep
   • Difficulty with nightmares

5. INTELLECTUAL
   • Poor concentration
   • Memory Impairment

6. DEPRESSED MOOD
   • Decreased interest
     in activities
   • Anhedoni
   • Insomnia

7. SOMATIC COMPLAINTS: MUSCULAR
   • Muscle aches or pains
   • Bruxism

8. SOMATIC COMPLAINTS: SENSORY
   • Tinnitus
   • Blurred vision

Score _____

☐ 9. CARDIOVASCULAR
       SYMPTOMS
       • Tachycardia
       • Palpitations
       • Chest pain
       • Sensation of feeling faint

☐ 10. RESPIRATORY
       SYMPTOMS
       • Chest pressure
       • Choking sensation
       • Shortness of breath

☐ 11. GASTROINTESTINAL
       SYMPTOMS
       • Dysphagia
       • Nausea or vomiting
       • Constipation
       • Weight loss
       • Abdominal fullness

☐ 12. GENITOURINARY
       SYMPTOMS
       • Urinary frequency
         or urgency
       • Dysmenorrhea
       • Impotence

☐ 13. AUTONOMIC
       SYMPTOMS
       • Dry mouth
       • Flushing
       • Pallor
       • Sweating

☐ 14. BEHAVIOR AT
       INTERVIEW
       • Fidgets
       • Tremor
       • Paces

References

Burns, D. (1999). , Rev. ed. *The feeling good handbook*, New York, NY, US: Plume/Penguin Books.

Damon, W. & Hart, D. (1988). *Self-understanding in childhood and adolescence.* Cambridge: Cambridge University Press.

Emler, N. (2002). The *costs and causes of low self-esteem.* Youth Studies Australia, 21(3), 45-48.

Gerondi, Rabbeinu Yonah, circa 1250.

Gray-Little, B., Williams, V.S.L., & Hancock, T. D. (1997). An item response theory analysis of the Rosenberg Self-Esteem Scale. Personality and Social Psychology Bulletin, 23, 443-451.

James, William, (1897). *The Will to Believe and Other Essays*, New York.

Lamden, E. (2006). *Torah Therapy: A guide to therapy in the spirit of Torah.* Jerusalem: Feldheim Publishers.

Lieberman, D. (2008). *Real Power: Rise above your nature and never feel angry, anxious, or insecure again.* Lakewood, NJ: Viters Press.

Marcia, J. (1966). *Development and validation of ego identity status. Journal of personality and Social Psychology.* 35:551-558

Mahler, M. F. Pine, and A. Bergman. (1975). *The psychological birth of the human infant.* New York: Basic Books

McDowell, I. (2006). Measuring health: A guide to rating scales and questionnaires (3rd ed.). New York: Oxford University Press.

Nave, C., Sherman, R., et. al., On the Contextual Independence of Personality: Teachers' Assessments Predict Directly Observed Behavior After Four Decades. Social Psychological and Personality Science, vol. 1, 4: pp. 327-334.

Spero, S. (2004). *What is Self-Theory and Does Judaism Need One?* The Torah U-Madda Journal, Vol. 12 (2004), pp. 130-157

Mead, G. H. (1934). *Mind, self, and society.* Chicago: University of Chicago Press.

Talmud, Tractate Brachot

Tracy, J., Cheng, J., Robins, R., and Trzesniewski, K. (2009). *Authentic and hubristic pride: the affective core of self-esteem and narcissism.* Self And Identity, *Vol.* 8, 2-3

Zeigler-Hill, V., Holden, C. J., Southard, A.C., Noser, A.E., Enjaian, B., & Pollack, N. C. (2016). *The dark sides of high and low self-esteem.* Science and Practice in Social, Personality, and Clinical Psychology, 325-40.

About the Authors

- YISROEL ROLL -

Yisroel Roll, MS, LCPC, JD, is a dynamic motivational speaker and a psychotherapist specializing in overcoming anxiety. He has lectured in Canada, the USA, England, South Africa and Israel. He is an Orthodox rabbi and served as the Rabbi of New West End Synagogue in London, England.

He serves as Scholar in Residence for retreats and seminars on themes including: Positive Parenting, The Self Confidence Seminar, Building Self Esteem in Ourselves and our Children, Seven Habits of Highly Happy People and Overcoming Anxiety.

His other books are:

> *Inner Peace—Achieving Self Esteem through Prayer*
> *Bring out the Best—the Jewish Guide to Building Family Esteem*
> *When the Going Gets Tough—Dealing with Life's Ups and Downs*
> *Step up to the Plate—Judaism, Baseball and How to Win the Game of Life*
> *Like Yourself and Your Spouse Will Too—The Key to Marriage Success*
> *Happiness is a Verb - How to Create Joy in your Life*
> *Self Esteem in the Talmud-the Pathways to Self Confidence and Resilience*
> *Alone Against the World—the Torah Antidote to Loneliness*

Yisroel Roll can be reached at yisroelroll@gmail.com.
www.yisroelroll.com

- MICHAEL LOCKMAN -

Michael Lockman, LCPC, is a mental health provider at the Cedar Ridge Counseling Center in Owings Mills, Maryland and specializes in helping clients who are struggling with grief and depression.He is presently earning certification in trauma-informed care. Lockman favors a spiritually-informed approach to counseling. He encourages clients to realize that their heartaches are really challenges that are tailor-made for their lives; trials designed to help each person self-actualize and come closer to God.

.

Made in the USA
Middletown, DE
30 June 2018